TOSHIKO MORI ARCHITECT

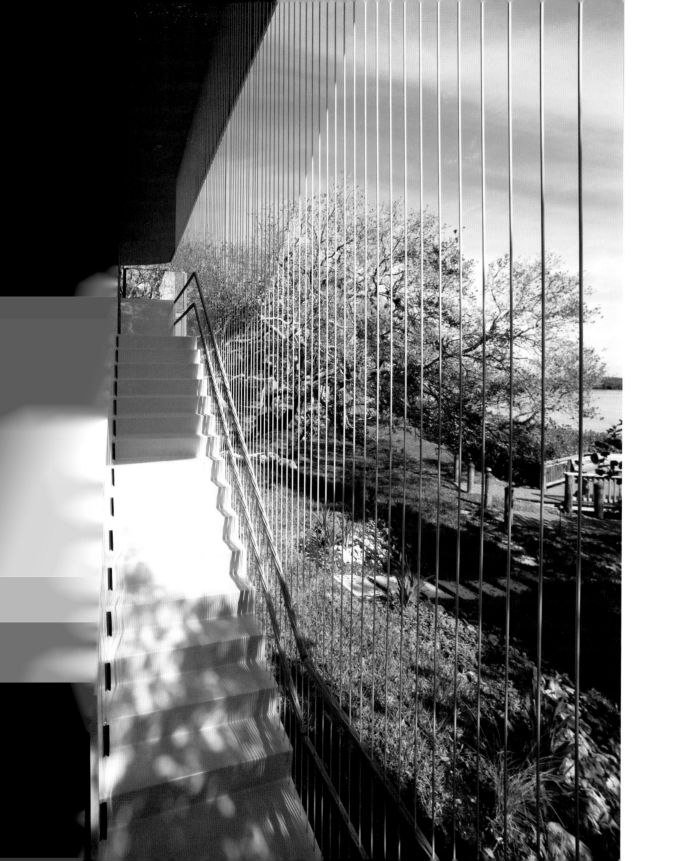

TOSHIKO MORI ARCHITECT

Foreword by K. Michael Hays

The Monacelli Press

First published in the United States of America in 2008 by
The Monacelli Press, Inc.
611 Broadway, New York, New York 10012

Library of Congress Cataloging-in-Publication Data
Toshiko Mori Architect (Firm).
Toshiko Mori Architect / foreword by K. Michael Hays.
p. cm.
ISBN 978-1-58093-191-5
1. Toshiko Mori Architect (Firm). 2. Architecture, Modern—20th century. 3. Architecture, Modern—21st century. I. Title.
NA737.T56A4 2008
720.92′2—dc22   2007032044

Printed and bound in China

Designed by Lorraine Wild and Robert Ruehlman with Victor Hu

CONTENTS

HISTORY/PRECEDENT

MATERIAL

SITE/CLIMATE

We have been taught to value an architecture of ideas—perhaps especially we who are the generation taught by Peter Eisenman, Aldo Rossi, John Hejduk, and others who through pedagogy and design practice developed an entirely new intellectual infrastructure and cultural vocation for architecture. And we have also learned that an architecture of ideas can exist only through an architecture of sense—a material expression that evokes a feeling in us. An architecture of sense is what happens when the formal codes of architecture meet the world of substances and experiences, when we open ourselves to the full force of new ways of thinking and feeling that are harnessed in perception. The question of our time, then, is one of sensibility—the presentation of an idea as a sensible experience. And the work of Toshiko Mori Architect offers an architecture of vastly expanded sensibility.

As soon as we recognize that concepts require materials for their comprehension (and that language is only one such material), we are in the realm of theory, that exhilarating but vexed territory bequeathed to us by our intellectual precursors. The excitement over theory was the inevitable and correct response to the valuation of an architecture of ideas, and the most advanced design practices since have tended to take on the categories and concepts of theory as their guides. But the response was one-sided, for in its excitement over concepts, theory seems to have developed a phobia for a language of sentiments that might register the desires and pleasures of things, images, and experiences. To read architecture as an isomorph of the categories and operations of theory can be as reductive as those readings that trace architecture to an inevitable reflection of a wholly predictable technological or economic context, that give no reciprocal force to architecture's untheorized affects. In our successful theorizing of ideas we have theorized ourselves out of the means to see architecture as exceeding our theories. Herein lies the importance of Toshiko Mori's expanded sensibility—an architecture of affects that develops and exceeds the architecture of ideas, that doesn't precede from theory so much as it proceeds *toward* new conceptualizations.

In general, affect is the changing intensity of specific (but often inexplicable) artistic properties (rhythm, texture, juxtaposition, coloring, and so forth)—the fear in a good ghost story that is produced not by the story's content but by the cadence and acoustics of the sentences, for example, or the anticipation in a dramatic film created by camera angles and cuts, or the shifting moods in a musical melody that are derived from different phrasings. An affect is the result of a sensation plus perception and as such it arrives *before* the idea that may or may not follow as a result of further conceptualization. Affect is libidinal before it is intellectual, bodily before theoretical. And it is therefore fundamentally forward-directed, an active potential of becoming-otherwise that may lead to further conceptualizations and theorizations down the line.

Take Mori's recurrent float-and-glow motif, for example, which appears in the work in different forms, from the earliest boutiques through to the extraordinary Salzburg Sternbrauerei housing competition. The effect of polished masses hovering backlit, surrounded by an inexplicable aura, is to push the main architectural elements toward extreme abstraction (any realist verisimilitude of load-bearing or enclosing function is evaporated) and to afford them the status of a recessive frame, platform, supporting surface, or matrix. Yet at the same time, the architecture is more *present*, more intimately *with us* than ever before. Architecture becomes body and body becomes architecture because the affect is not merely that of moving bodies through space but of the architectural body as an expression and figure of the force of movement itself—movement made sensible by becoming material in a particularly architectural way.

Or consider the shifting, sliding, rotating volumes of the studio's residential projects, which begin as spatial distributions of program and circulation but then dissolve into the sensible effects of materials like microlouvered glass of varying transparencies, textured wood and fabric screens, and recycled aluminum foam planks; of environmental technologies like geothermal heating systems and photovoltaic patches; even of contexts and histories—Breuer and Rudolph, vistas and vegetation, and the unique, sustainable beauty of the sites. Affect works on multiple and heterogeneous levels, cutting across zones that intellection alone would hold separate. Therefore the extreme contrast of the precise, minimal plan drawings and the delightful richness of the completed structures is no accident, for the plans and the buildings themselves are but diagrams that organize perpetually changing affects.

Affect is analogic and expansive, not digital or discrete. Affects are sensible in their singularity—a totality of sensation that cannot be summed up or figured out. They are sensible rather than intelligible, liberated from organizing conceptual systems of meaning and representation, then condensed into the mood and moment of an event. They achieve their effect through bodily perceptions, but they are not identical to the particular bodies or subjects that experience them. They are properties of objects. So each of us may perceive them differently and may return and experience them anew.

There is more. Mori's moods are irreducibly architectural not because their content is architectural but because the particular sensible forces with which they produce experience are derived from the discipline and techniques of architecture. Whence, too, comes the pleasure with which they are apprehended. For we have had similar experiences before—Lissitzky's Prouns hovering in luminescent midair; Barnett Newman's "zips," whose layered translucencies transcend meaningful messages, messengers, and memories all through their immediate and self-reflexive address; Mies's trabeated whisper, the barely enunciated horizontal-vertical mark of load bearing whose aural minimalism is itself exceeded in the diagrid of Mori's Salzburg Sky Dwelling as it almost disappears into the echo of the cliff's pattern; Hejduk's obsessive-compulsive precision, which attained paradoxically surreal effects. But all these, too, are disrupted in Mori's refusal to reduce the architectural encounter to concepts and clichés already known.

What is preserved is a block of sensations, percepts, and affects. Toshiko Mori Architect constructs well-tempered environments replete with modulations, shades, variations of atmosphere, multiple encounters, and nuances that thicken the situation, slow down movement, and are nevertheless exquisitely apprehensible. They are passageways of experience and thought that produce life-enhancing enjoyments.

INTRODUCTION
TOSHIKO MORI

Every work of architecture is a manifesto. With each work, we architects reassess the meaning of what we have proposed. Every project is a rare opportunity to voice our ideas and concepts. In ways small and large, in the private sector or the public realm, and eventually through the body of our works, both the grandiose and the humble become physical reality. Unlike art, music, or literature, architecture is tied to a location and a program; it is never separate from its context. It is simultaneously protagonist and antagonist. When a building is inhabited, ideas are transmitted on a daily basis, slowly seeping into the lives of its occupants. In its omnipresence, architecture is probably the most subversive form of art.

The architect's concern is environment and space. Architecture is an art of imagination and observation, both crucial faculties. The rich possibilities of expression must balance the analytical and objective reading of meanings and effects. In our practice, material, fabrication, and performance are the recurring research techniques we use to develop buildings that are both precise in function and imprecise in poetic atmosphere. Likewise, the organizing topics of this book—History/Precedent, Material, and Site/Climate—outline strategies that engage our work with a broader discussion of architecture. In our design process, we move back and forth between materials, modes of fabrication, and building performance, which includes sustainability, climate and site considerations, and maintenance. Inevitably all of the strategies and themes interact, though for some projects one theme may be more dominant.

Because it is an enduring and practical form of art, architecture is a powerful and exact method of conveying thought. At times, architecture makes a grand statement, loudly voicing its presence and reason for existence. But often it provides a background whisper for daily dramas. Memories are often associated with particulars of location: the look of the surrounding space, the quality of the light. This powerful associative capacity has been abused, as when built form is appropriated as propaganda, and even today architecture is used as the armature of commercial advertisements. As architects, we must put forth an extra effort to offer our ideas about what our work represents, our interpretation of the meaning. In architecture, the medium does become the message. Each project must invigorate the social and intellectual life of a greater public and also fulfill functional requirements and command a visual presence.

I owe this foundation for my work to my mentor, the late John Hejduk, dean of the School of Architecture at Cooper Union for twenty-five years. The way Hejduk thought about architecture had a profound effect on many architects of my generation. His fundamental ideas produced an influential group with powerful, vibrant voices. I attended Cooper as an undergraduate, and then I taught there for fourteen years. During that time, John instilled in me the importance of architecture's unique social contract: an unwritten trust between architect and society. Architects are important not only because we create buildings for shelter but because we offer a program, a distinct and creative mission for every project. From small houses to public institutions, each piece of built work is interwoven into the physical, ethical, and emotive fabric of civilization.

John Hejduk spoke often about another distinct characteristic of architecture, transferability. Architecture is an instrument that facilitates the transmission of ideas from one medium to another. By his definition, architecture can be a book, a drawing, an unrealized project. Furthermore, the concepts or ideas of architecture must transcend their built form, attaining a broader and more universal realm. If there is a primary challenge in my work as an architect, it can be distilled to this charge. The visitor center for Frank Lloyd Wright's Darwin D. Martin house, to give one example, exemplifies my interest in the relationship between size and scale. I wanted to challenge the notion that monumental equals large. The combination of glass perimeter walls and four interior piers supporting the inverted roof creates the appearance of an extreme cantilever. The pavilion is transparent and compact, yet it has a definitive presence that stands up against the sprawling house by Wright.

I use the idea of transferability to continually reevaluate our work as well as to generally assess the relevance of works of architecture today. Many architects articulate their projects in a way that supports a precise viewpoint. But the discipline of architects lies in the many ways a constructed work can manifest itself. There is a huge gap between scale drawings, study models, and renderings and the physicality of the constructed work. Different scales—global and urban, macroscopic and microscopic—generate differentiated and calibrated discourses. How can we sharpen our powers of imagination to predict the outcome and at the same time allow for the essential quality of any architecture to come to life?

The process of design is an incessant imagining and reimagining of the permutations of materials and methods of assembly and their effects. If a concept is transferable and attains universal understanding, the material character of the resulting building generates a unique vocabulary that is specific to its site. I strive to capture a certain atmosphere of site and program, a genius loci or essential spirit. Perhaps it is an effort to seek the spiritual dimension in architecture. For the house in Chatham, for example, we originally proposed a cladding of black carbon fiber that varied in width and depth of corrugation, creating a dispersed perceptual focus. We thought that preventing the eye from quite focusing on details and form would initiate a contrast between the clear geometry of the house and a blur at the surface and edges, narrowing the pictorial gap between nature and artifice. In the end, we selected a cladding of recycled aluminum foam. The foam will refract sunlight, creating a similar effect through light diffusion rather than human perception. The matte-silver aluminum will appear more atmospheric and ethereal than the black carbon fiber.

Syracuse Center of Excellence
in Environmental and
Energy Systems

In architecture, there is an essential quality to be captured in each project. A carefully researched
and elaborately argued process usually produces one indisputable solution. In our work, clarity
of intent is backed by a complex and layered agenda. Our work is simple in its appearance, yet
it has multiple narratives, analytical and spiritual, interwoven within. In architecture, such narratives unfold slowly; time is required for perception and observation. Designing buildings therefore
requires many storylines, each unfolding at its own pace. One story may unfold for one observer
while different ideas come to light for another. In this way the complexity of the building's purpose
is preserved. Rafael Moneo said in 1986, "I like to see the building assume its proper condition, living its own life. Therefore, I do not believe that architecture is just the superstructure that we intro-
duce when we talk about buildings. I prefer to think that architecture is the air we breathe when
buildings have arrived at their radical solitude." Yet many buildings are static and isolated when
they are built, rather than silent yet alive in their solitude. The building itself is a final product; it
does not have the life force required to become part of the life of the occupant, the site, the city. If
architecture is to enter the fabric of society, it must attain its own identity and character as one element in the civic chorus.

Certain techniques fold our ideas into the design process analytically rather than metaphorically.
In the early stages of work, there is a direct correspondence between thoughts and drawings. To
saturate architecture with variable concepts, our design tools are the techniques of building: structure, material assembly, detailing, juxtaposition of surfaces and textures, consideration of assembly,
investigation of environmental aspects. These techniques are an extension of methods learned in

early drawing lessons: for both, visual literacy is the faculty that balances and calibrates the project. The unique characteristics of the medium or material, the balance of the composition, and the degree of abstraction: all leave a trace. No matter how complex or how sophisticated the technologies, we continue a nuanced process to re-present these challenges of poetic understanding to the realm of architecture.

The Syracuse Center of Excellence in Environmental and Energy Systems, for example, is a highly technical building, and its primary focus is building performance, specifically energy efficiency, sustainability, and indoor environmental quality. The various programs are interwoven in section. The transparent tower, containing environmental quality labs that measure human comfort, and the opaque "tail," which encloses materials labs under a green roof, intersect at the place of learning. The classrooms extend the artificial nature of the green roof, and two sets of testing labs flanking the classrooms express an attempt to create balance between nature and artifice.

Architecture is a noble profession, and ultimately it exists to improve the quality of life. Each opportunity we are given to build a project, we take as a gift. In return, we engage with each project with compassion, attempting to capture an ethereal vision that will carry it into the future. It is strange that what we do should be valid for many years to come yet must be of its own moment. Architecture survives its architects. I often think of buildings as they evolve: the passage of time, change of ownership, and modification of function. (This is the reverse of the *firmitas* that is usually attributed to historic buildings.) What will be the ultimate footprint of the structures? These are the existential thoughts that occur as I design, as I keep in mind the essential properties of each building.

My life as an architect has been slow and incremental. There is a toughness required to execute projects, to give each its own life. Resilience and the "Teflon effect" are vital attributes. Architects cannot be defeated by disappointments. The profession requires mental strength, good health, and especially a strong stomach. An unlimited amount of optimism, a healthy dose of idealism, and high energy and high spirits help us to persevere through difficult circumstances. Late nights of self-doubt and self-critique raise questions of means and intent; these moments, which are held over from student days, create necessary momentum to move further, to create challenges and to formulate new questions. In fact, these moments are also the most productive and valuable time of reflection.

In this little book—and for good reason—we shall repeat again and again that we are not studying the creative phenomenon but one of the possible material supports of creative thought.
—Le Corbusier, *Modulor 2*, 1955

There is no innovation without history. In all of our projects, we are in active dialogue with the precedents to our work, be they events or architecture: the writings of Edgar Allan Poe, the artworks of Josef and Anni Albers, iconic buildings by Frank Lloyd Wright, Marcel Breuer, and Paul Rudolph. Through an analysis of history, we synthesize site, function, and climate into the program we create for each project. We place our new work in contrast— not in opposition or in imitation—to the history and context; we attempt to tread the fine line between reinvention and reference, a strategy we call regenerative practice.

Our work endeavors to add the spatial promise of architecture to the factual flatness of history. We try to distill the essential quality of the original work and infuse the abstract of its story into new ideas to generate vitality for the future. While our work suggests new interpretations, it proposes continuity rather than disruption. We strive toward a delicate balance between appreciation for the past and creation of a fresh discourse.

HISTORY/
PRECEDENT

House on the Gulf of Mexico I, Casey Key, Florida, 1999. Sited on a 535-foot-wide sandbar near Sarasota, Florida, with the Gulf of Mexico to the west and Little Sarasota Bay to the east, this guest house complements a 1957 residence designed by Paul Rudolph. The design is a tribute to the legacy of the Sarasota school, a group of architects led by Rudolph and Ralph Twitchell, who practiced in the area from the early 1940s through the mid-1960s. The house regenerates the tropical modernist style and vocabulary of their work—protective roof planes, concrete blocks—yet takes into consideration severe climate and site requirements, evolving the modernist paradigm into one that is more harmonious with the surrounding environment.

The densely planted site is subject to extreme climatic events—hurricanes, floods, downpours, strong sun, and constant exposure to salt. In addition, the gulf side is a protected sea turtle habitat; the bay side, a protected manatee habitat. The guest house, built on the footprint of an older building destroyed by hurricanes, is raised seventeen feet above sea level to protect from future storm surges and flooding. Construction techniques likewise respond to the exigencies of the climate. Concrete foundation piles are driven twenty-one feet into the sand; concrete grade beams and pile caps support cast-in-place piers; and floor slabs, also poured-in-place concrete, are supported by concrete masonry shear walls and tubular steel columns.

The flora of the site—live oaks, palms, and mangroves—was equally important in designing the guest house. The bulk of the building is within the dense tree canopy, which offers privacy and shade. The pilotis that support the habitable space above wave-crest height respond to tree trunks. An exterior stainless-steel staircase provides access to the living areas. The stair becomes the new center of the house, connecting and separating the activities within. Window frames are steel; glazing is clear, opaque, or translucent as appropriate to protect from solar glare and heat gain and minimize cooling needs.

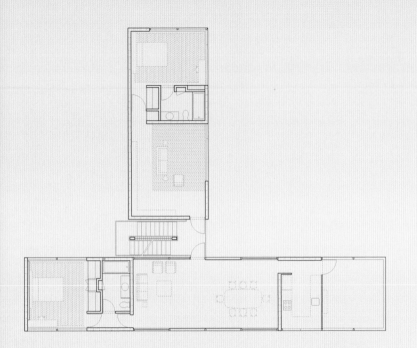

First Level Plan

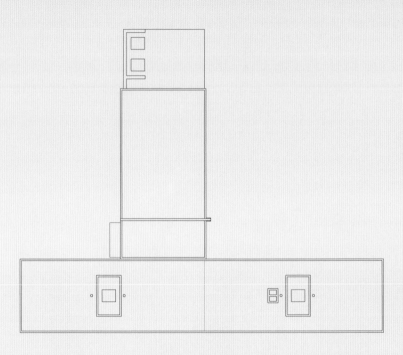

Roof Plan

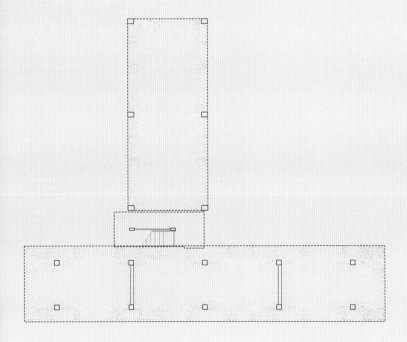

Ground Level Plan

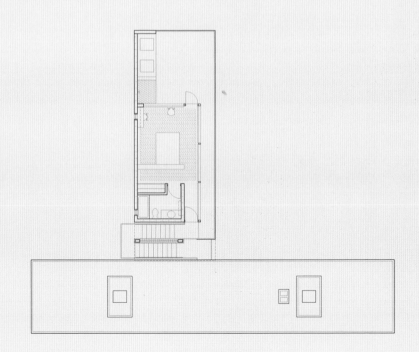

Second Level Plan

0   20 feet

Frank Lloyd Wright's Darwin D. Martin House Complex Visitor Center, Buffalo, New York, 2008. The visitor center houses gallery, orientation, and gathering spaces for the Darwin D. Martin House, a residential compound built by Frank Lloyd Wright in 1906. Our design strategy creates a dialogue with the Martin House through contrast rather than imitation. Though small in size, the visitor center is afforded a monumental quality through its simplicity and clarity. Reinterpreting Wright's lifelong attention to exploring materials, technologies, and techniques, the new building reflects the structural, infrastructural, and programmatic relationships of the Martin House in a contemporary and abstract design.

The inverted hipped roof of the visitor center refers to the form of Wright's building while simultaneously marking its distinct public function. The glass facade and open plan of the new construction similarly contrast with the introversion of Wright's design. The module of the center is determined by a projection of the spacing of the pergola that connects the original Martin House to the outbuildings. In this way, the new building also relates to the garden, and the renovated pergola is newly resonant.

The visitor center translates Wright's organic architecture into a vocabulary of sustainable principles in consideration not only of contemporary environmental concerns but of Wright's interest in technological innovation. Geothermal heating and displacement ventilation minimize long-term energy costs. Perimeter mullions are structural, supporting the building's lateral load. Infrastructure is integrated at the center bay of the four structural piers, consolidating building services.

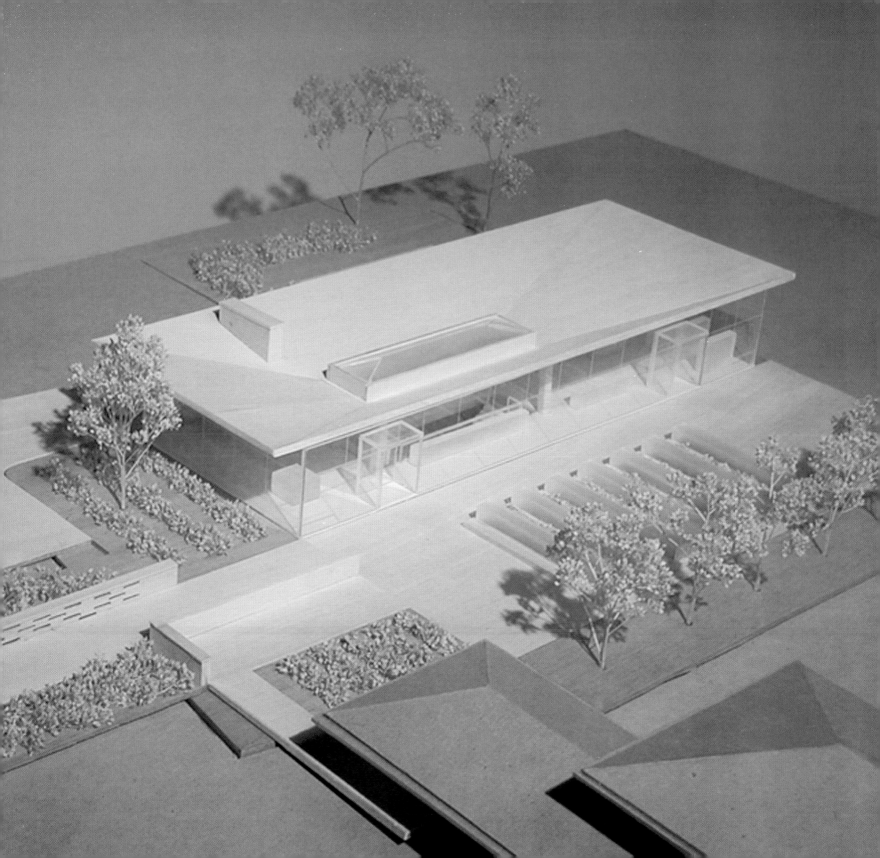

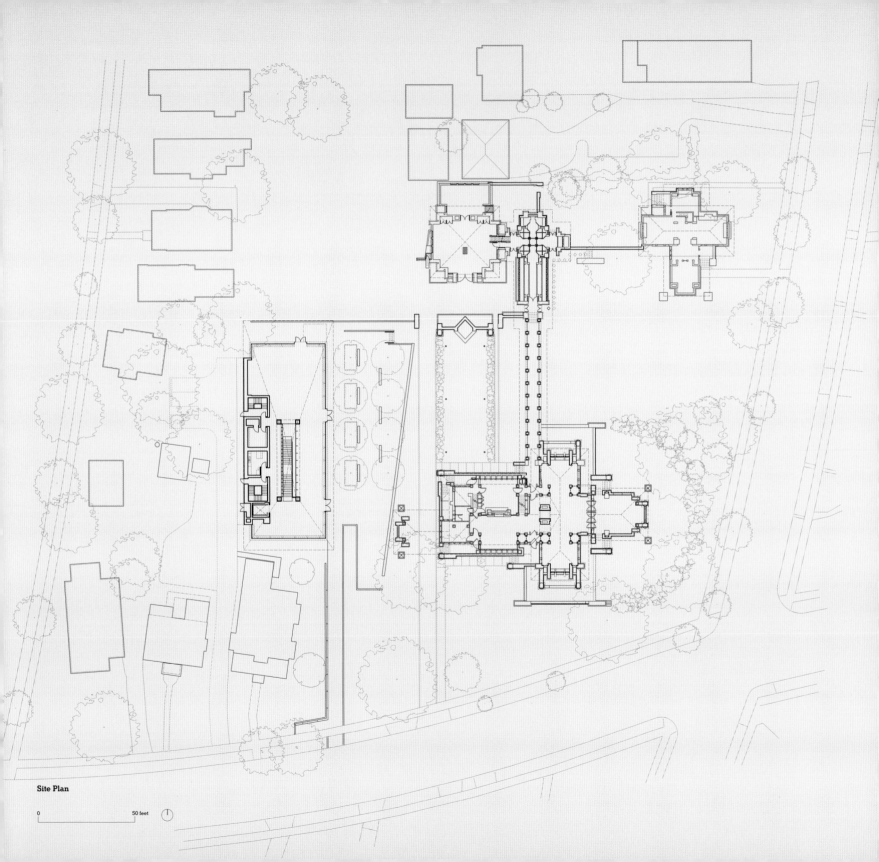

Site Plan

0   50 feet

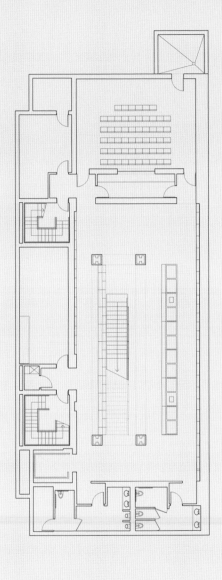

Lower Level Plan

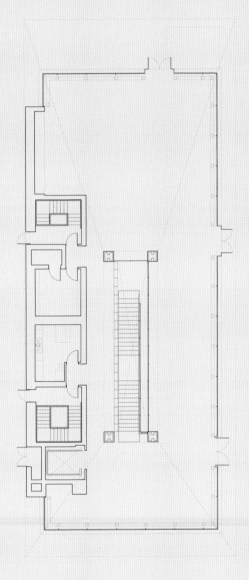

Main Level Plan

Roof Plan

0   25 feet

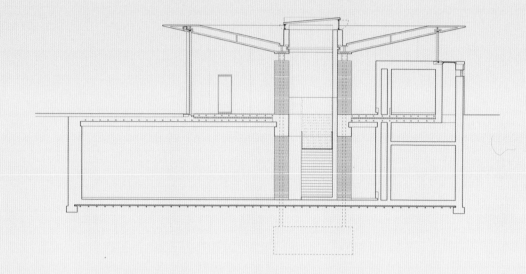

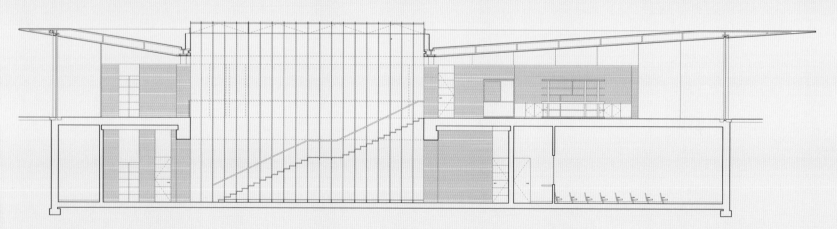

Sections

0   25 feet

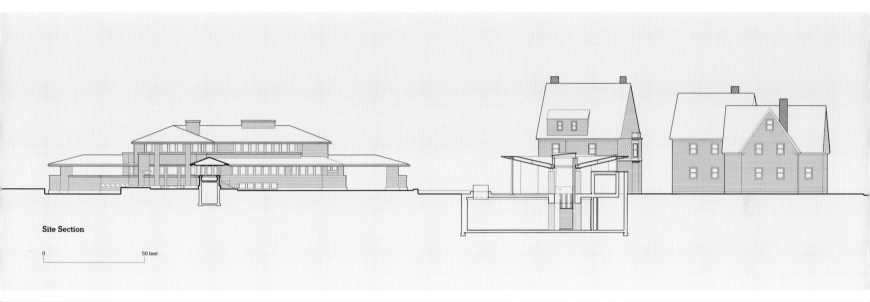

Site Section

0   50 feet

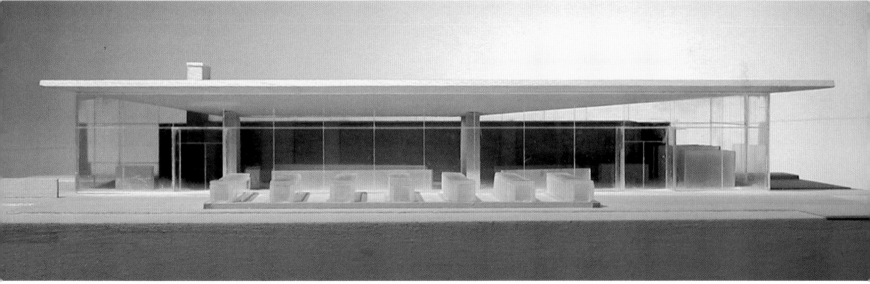

House in Connecticut II, New Canaan, Connecticut, 2008.

In 1951, Marcel Breuer designed a house in New Canaan for himself and his family. More than fifty years (and one expansion) later, we are renovating the residence to preserve the spirit of Breuer's design and, at the same time, to update the space to accommodate a contemporary family. The original house contains living and dining areas, family room, and kitchen, and an addition houses the master bedroom suite and two bedrooms on the upper level and utility space (garage and mud room) on the lower level. The addition is joined to the Breuer residence by a connecting stair enclosed in glass of varying transparency.

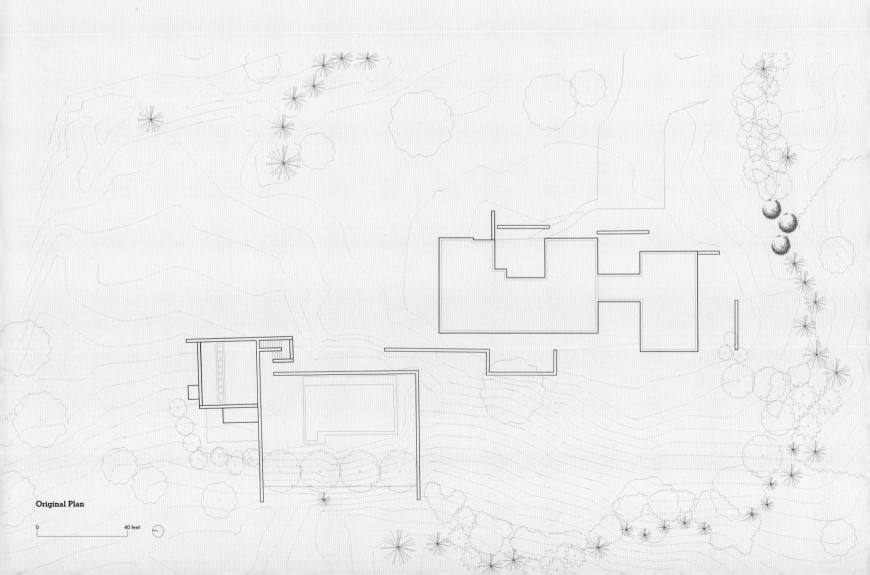

Original Plan

0   40 feet

In the original house, the floors and walls of local bluestone are restored to maintain the character. A new clerestory at the roof brings more light into the compressed volume and reinstates, in its shape and position, the primary circulation path of Breuer's 1951 design. This skylight also relates to the light-filled addition and the connecting stair.

The relationship between the existing house and the addition expresses the contrast between heavy and light in both material and form. While the original structure is composed primarily of heavy stone walls and large expanses of glass, the addition proposes a material palette of finer gradation and more innovative application. The facade of the upper volume alternates clear, translucent, and opaque glass in a pattern that reflects the interior functions. The lower level is clad in slender stone "louvers" that float three inches from the facade, rendering light and screenlike

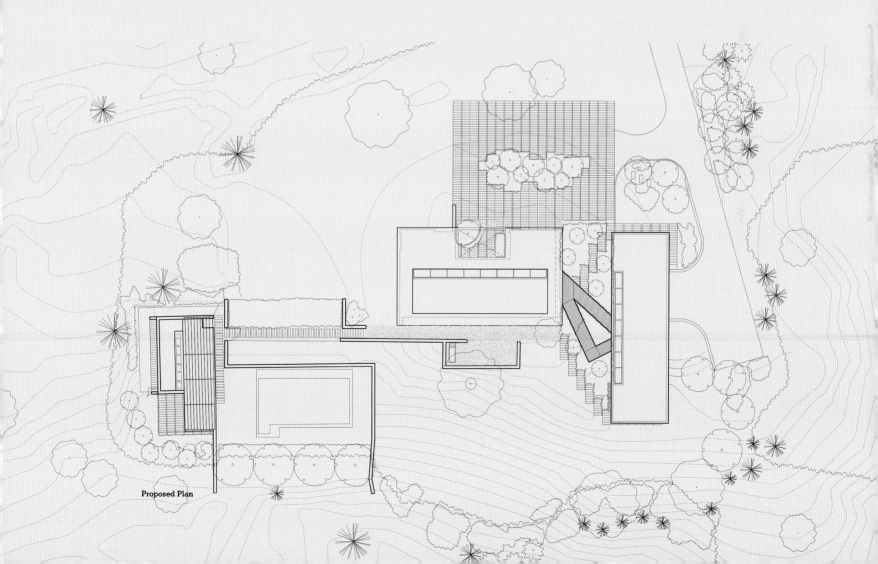

Proposed Plan

a material usually associated with weight and opacity. Large cantilevers to the east and west allow the new building to hover next to the older house, which is more horizontal and grounded; the lower level of the addition is sunk four feet into the ground, preventing it from overpowering the modest proportions of Breuer's residence.

Even as the addition takes its cues from the orthogonal lines and limited dimensions of the existing house, the stair connector departs from this geometry. Positioned between the two volumes and slipping diagonally into a preexisting opening in the original house, the stair acts as both bridge and break between old and new, connecting to each but belonging to neither. Toward the street, the stair is enclosed in translucent glass that offers privacy; on the opposite side, clear glass affords open sightlines between Breuer's original residence and our new design. Because the two-story addition has no internal stair, this connector daily integrates the experience of old and new.

Sustainable features—a particular interest of Breuer's—incorporated into the renovation will assure the continued longevity of the residence. The membrane roof of the existing structure contains photovoltaic "patches" that provide more than 30 percent of the electricity for the residence. Solar panels on the roof of the addition supply up to 70 percent of domestic hot water.

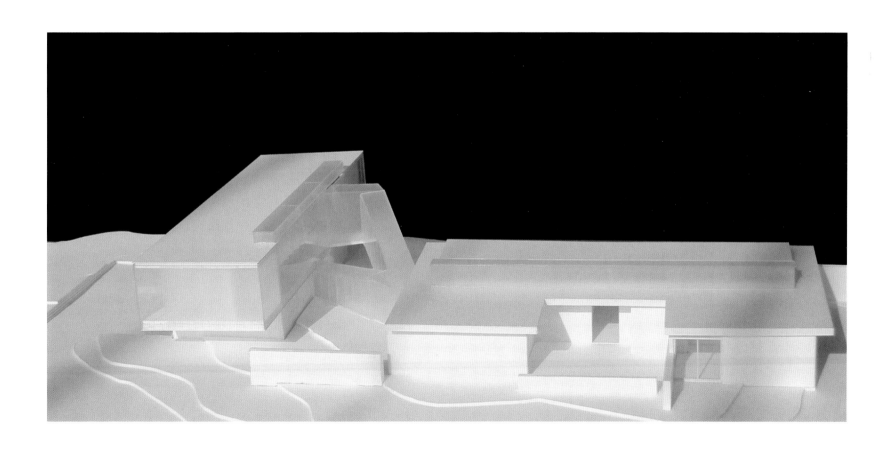

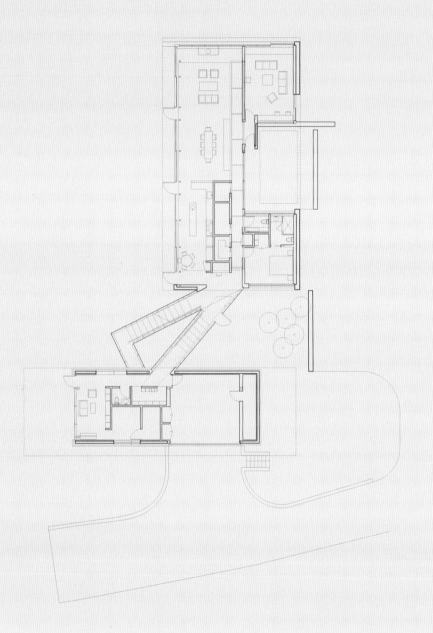

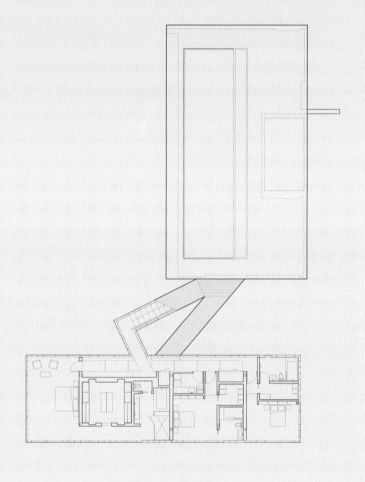

Lower Level Plan

Upper Level Plan

0   40 feet

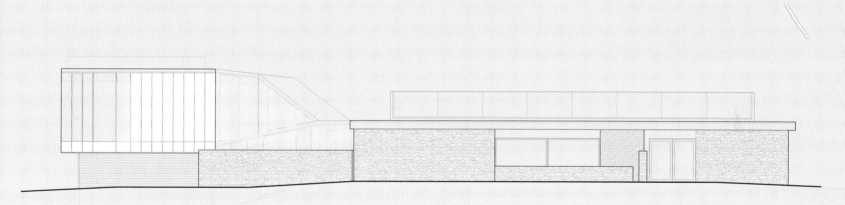

East Elevation

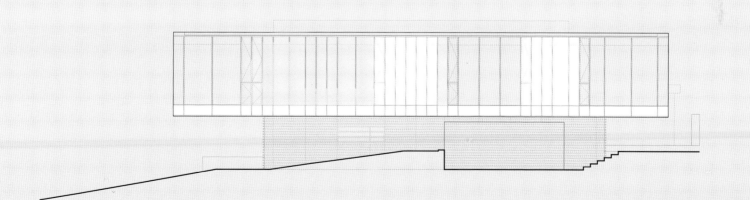

South Elevation

"Josef and Anni Albers: Designs for Living," Cooper-Hewitt, National Design Museum, New York, New York, 2004. The exhibit combines, for the first time, the textiles of Anni Albers and the furniture of Josef Albers. The exhibition is conceived as a series of dialogues between the two designers, juxtaposing their work from the early 1920s to the 1950s—from their Bauhaus years to their arrival in America—to understand how they influenced each other while still retaining artistic autonomy and to highlight the material and structural relationships evident in their designs. It is organized as a series of purely visual vignettes that create connections and contrasts between their work. The installation combines yet holds separate the work of two independent artists and at the same time reveals intimate connections experienced by the viewer.

At all times adhering to strict conservation standards, we suspended textiles, cantilevered horizontal display cases, and recessed vertical display cabinets. Lighting recesses at the top of the cases optimize viewing of intricate detail and reduce glare.

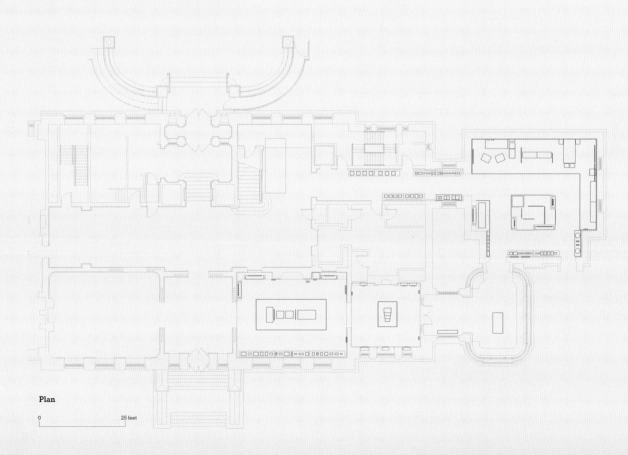

Plan

0   25 feet

JOSEF AND ANNI ALBERS
DESIGNS FOR LIVING

Josef and Anni Albers: Designs for Living has been organized by Cooper-Hewitt, National Design Museum, Smithsonian Institution, and the Josef and Anni Albers Foundation. Additional support was provided by Maharam.

Josef and Anni Albers Foundation Pavilion, Bethany, Connecticut, 2007. Wedged into a sloping site in the Connecticut woods, the Albers Foundation Pavilion displays the textiles of Anni Albers and the furniture, glass constructions, and drawings of Josef Albers, all part of the collection of the Josef and Anni Albers Foundation. The building, a translucent glass bar, contains exhibition vaults that modulate natural light and control climate for the sensitive works. Each vault is lined with a visible storage system so that visitors may easily access archived works. By collapsing storage and display into individual spaces, scholars can view important objects and immediately compare them to precedents. A reading room at the eastern end of the building allows artists-in-residence, scholars, and visitors a quiet place to study amid the surrounding woods.

    The pavilion's opaque exhibition chambers are set at various distances from the translucent facades, an homage to Josef Albers and his manipulation of perceived spatial depth. This interaction of surfaces is realized both spatially and experientially. In places where the Alberses' work is displayed, artificial light emanates from within; the opposite condition holds for the naturally lit perimeter circulation. By requiring visitors to navigate these liminal zones, the architecture seeks to inspire a fresh insight into the fundamental concepts of the works of Josef and Anni Albers.

Site Plan

0   100 feet

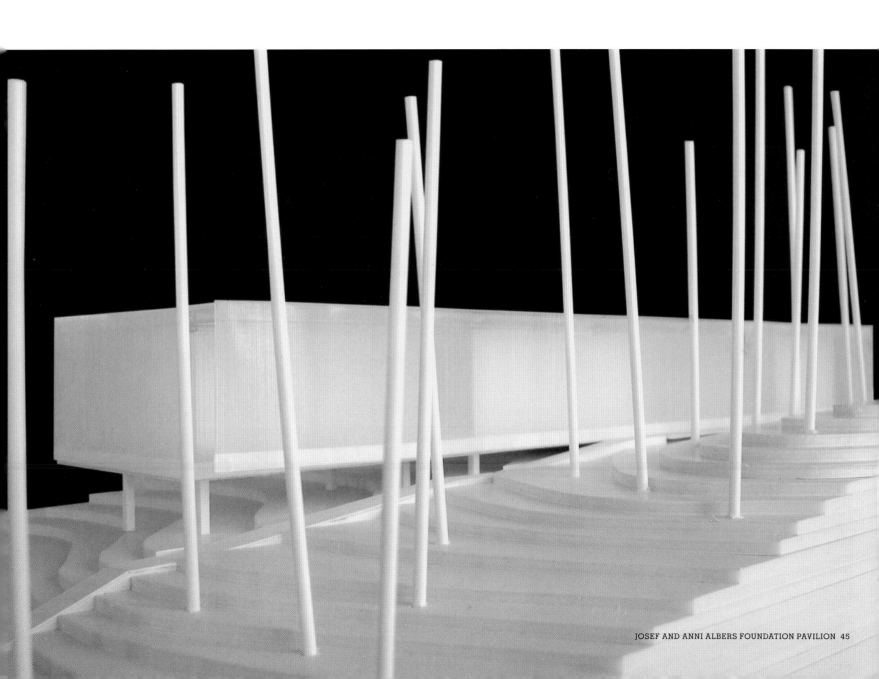

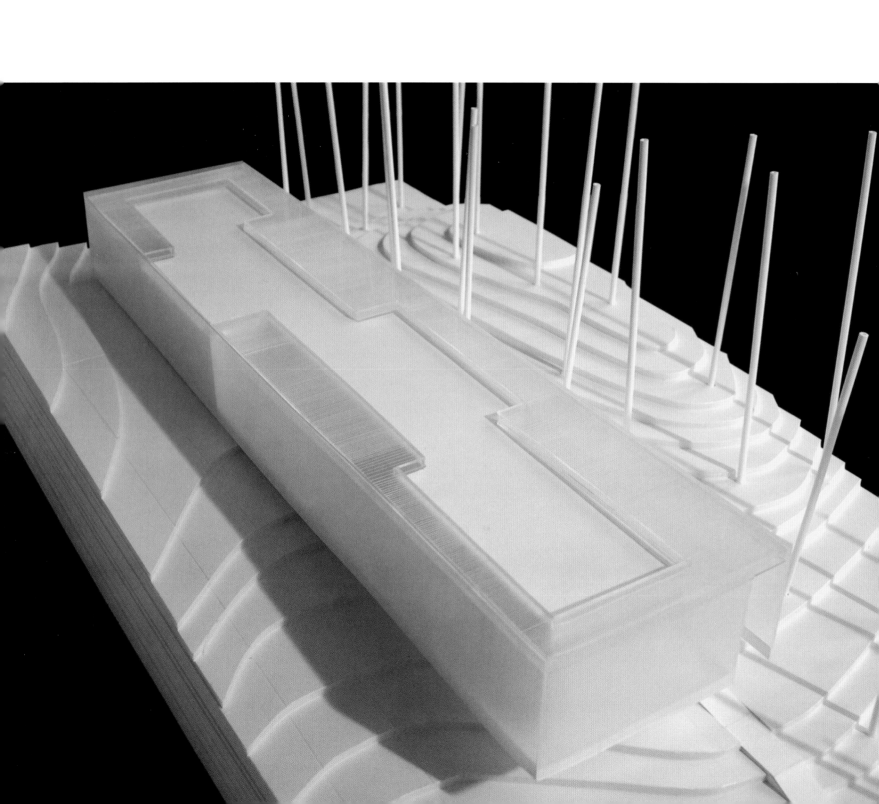

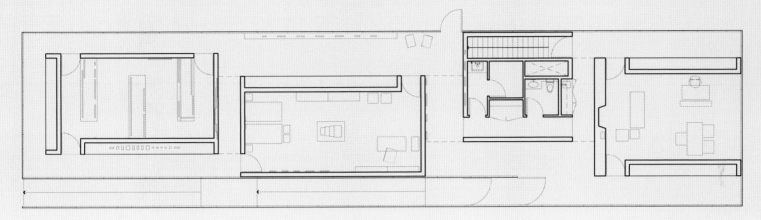

Upper Level Plan

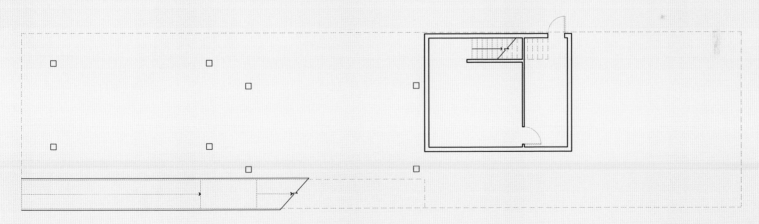

Lower Level Plan

0   15 feet

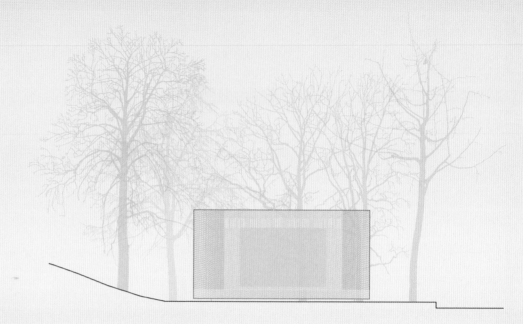

East Elevation

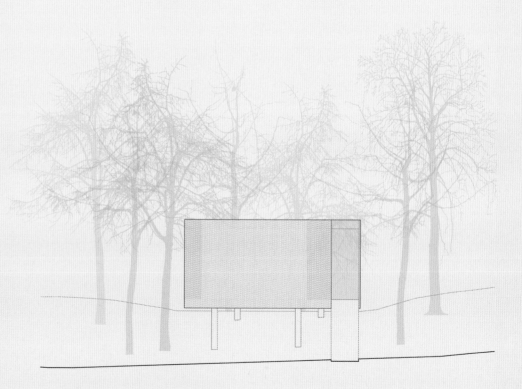

West Elevation

0   15 feet

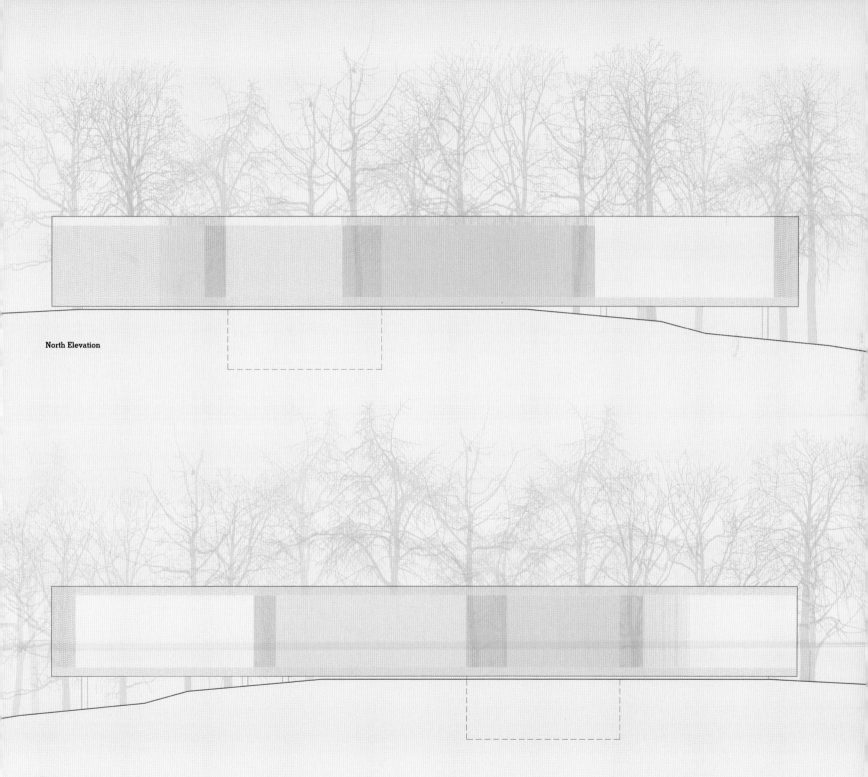

North Elevation

South Elevation

Jingxiangqingke Housing Project, Beijing, China, 2005. The Jingxiangqingke housing project suggests a housing type, unique for its location and the economic class of its inhabitants, that combines work and living spaces. The layout of the housing units reflects the diverse needs and desires of the occupants, who face a dramatic lifestyle shift as China undergoes enormous social and economic change. Within each unit, a "loose fit" design allows flexibility of use and program. Rooms are suitable for residential, commercial, and mixed uses and various styles of living. Exterior spaces are embedded into the rooms. The units, which allow varying degrees of privacy and separation between different functions, can comfortably house a family of multiple generations, thus restoring a traditional lifestyle to a country with rapid development.

　　　　In several related building forms, the customary house shape is faceted like a rock crystal to generate a new expression for the hybrid live-work typology. Cutting away the volume at the corners increases surface area, allowing opportunities for additional daylighting and ventilation. Differing views, access, and qualities of light and air give variety to the spaces.

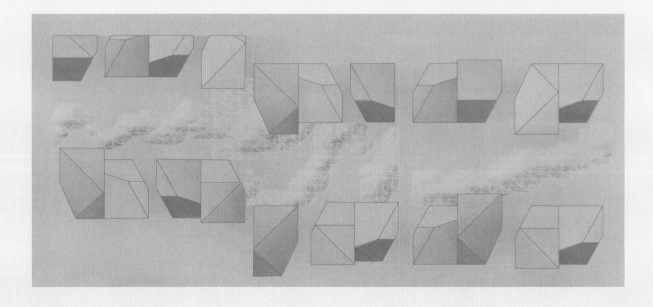

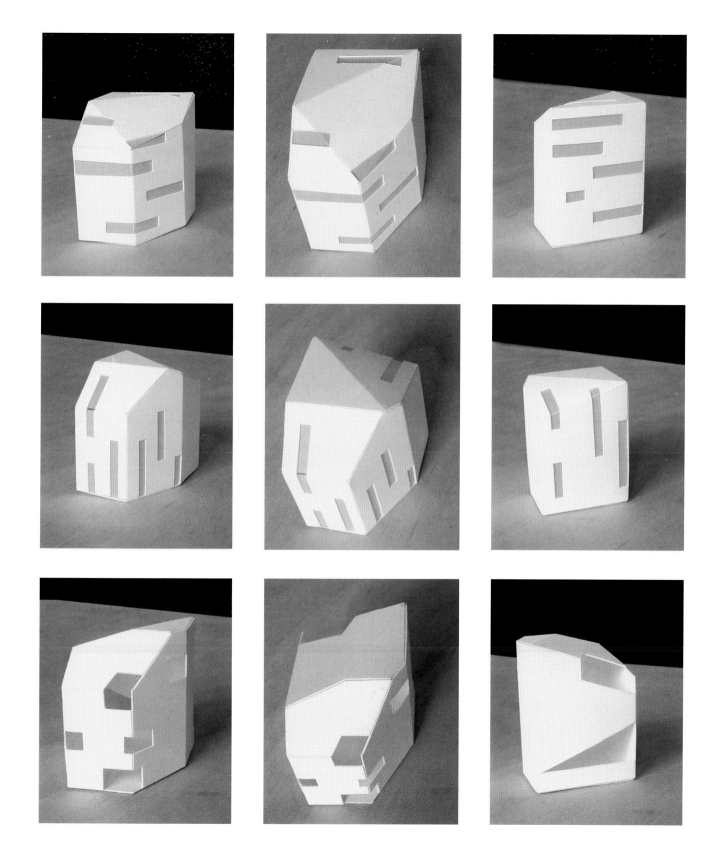

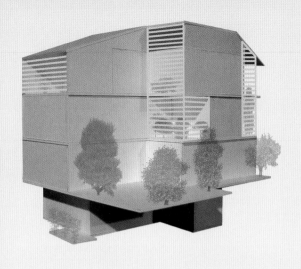
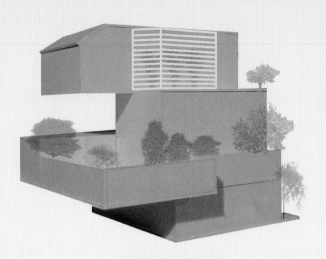
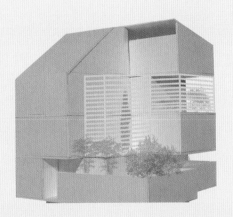
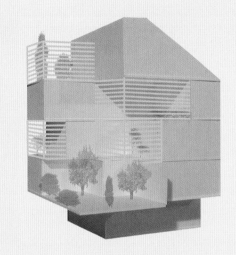

Unit Plans, Type J

The exterior cladding, an inexpensive indigenous gray slate, evokes traditional roofing materials. Here, the slate is applied across the entire structure, roof and walls, in an abstract pattern drawn from Chinese stonework. The subtle transition in pattern from ground to building and from floor to wall integrates interior, exterior, and landscape. The interiors are lined in wood to promote warm and tactile qualities. Colored ceramic tile, made with local techniques, accents walls and floors.

The recurring horizontal stratification on both the interior and the exterior refers to geologic layers. This modular woven tapestry gives richness and range to the design. The strata also coordinate alignment of doors, windows, shelving, and furniture for ease of construction. Horizontal wood louvers encourage the growth of climbing vines, which shade the exterior terraces and further integrate the housing units with the surrounding landscape. Instead of uniform repetition, this design strategy differentiates each unit; combined, the units create an informal and accidental pattern. This type of housing departs from convention to encourage individuated lifestyles and entrepreneurship.

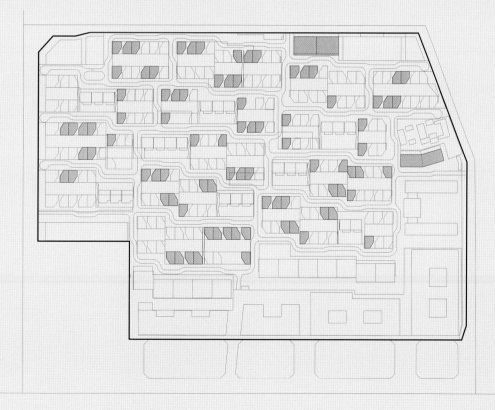

Site Plan

0   100 meters

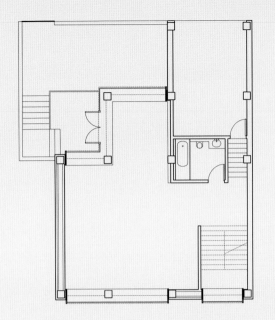

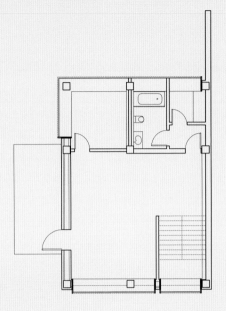

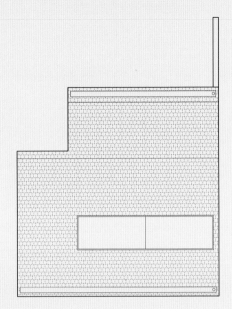

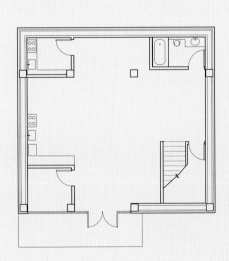

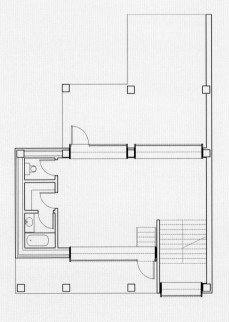

Unit Plans, Type J

0   5 meters

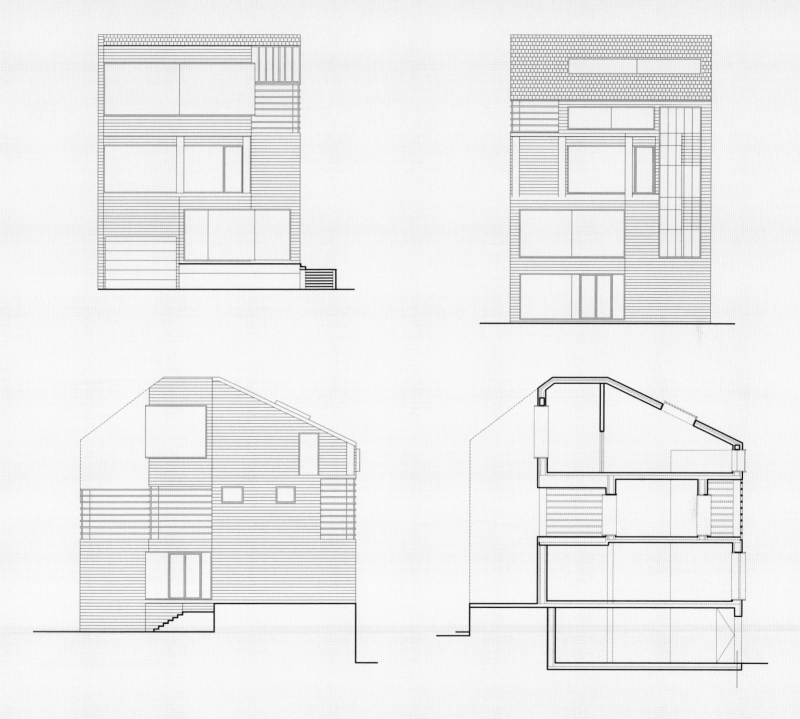

Elevations and Section, Type J

Landscape Plan

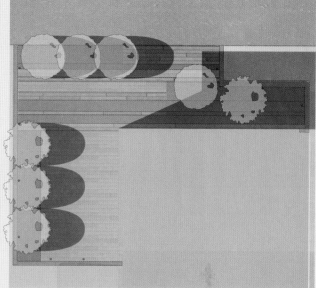

Winter

Summer

Loft in New York City, New York, New York, 2006. This 5,600-square-foot renovation reevaluates the typology of the classic New York City loft. We carefully considered the cavernous open space of the L-shaped loft, in view of the needs of the clients, who required public area to display art and entertain and private spaces for a growing family. The industrial space is scaled down to residential habitation, but it is not partitioned into rooms.

       The first of the two main zones retains the traditional characteristics of a loft—a large space defined not by walls but by freestanding pieces of furniture. Kitchen, living space, and children's play area, though defined in this way, still read as one expansive space. Extra-large built-in cabinets and storage spaces decrease the width of the open area. The second zone provides private spaces along the edge of the L. The library and media room, which fit into this zone, may be opened to the central space. Finally, a "solarium," which may be considered a third zone, takes advantage of a small span of southern exposure to bring sunlight into the darkest area of the loft.

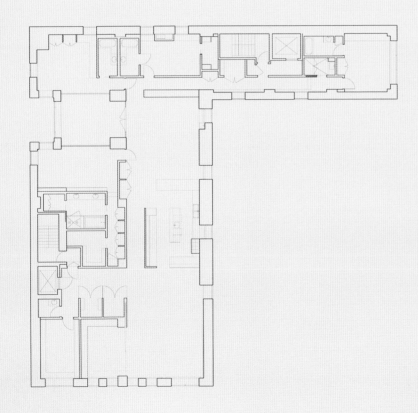

Plan

0   25 feet

Smithsonian Patent Office Building Courtyard Competition, Washington, D.C., 2003. The competition called for enclosing the courtyard of the Patent Office Building, which currently houses the Smithsonian American Art Museum and the National Portrait Gallery. The building, constructed in stages between 1836 and 1868, occupies a full block in Pierre Charles L'Enfant's 1791 plan for Washington, D.C. Our proposal envisions the courtyard, conceived by L'Enfant as a democratic "living room," as a new enclosed public space imbued with light and atmosphere. These have served as quintessential forces of inspiration throughout the history of American art. This project also exemplifies Jefferson's idea that innovation is an engine for a democratic society.

The new covering for the courtyard consists of two interdependent elements, a light filter and a diaphanous undulating glass-grid shell roof supporting it. Together these form a radiant, suspended plane of light visible throughout the city, a counterpoint to the reflecting pool on the National Mall. Operable louvers within the light filter provide daylighting control. The shell roof beneath is delicate in appearance yet extraordinarily structurally efficient. Its undulating lightness provides a contrast to the masonry vaulting of the original building.

A series of flexible architectural elements activates the courtyard; a programmable floor composed of wood and backlit glass produces different patterns underfoot. Acoustic screens modulate sounds, and movable planters and seating can be configured to orchestrate multiple functions.

SMITHSONIAN PATENT OFFICE BUILDING COURTYARD COMPETITION 63

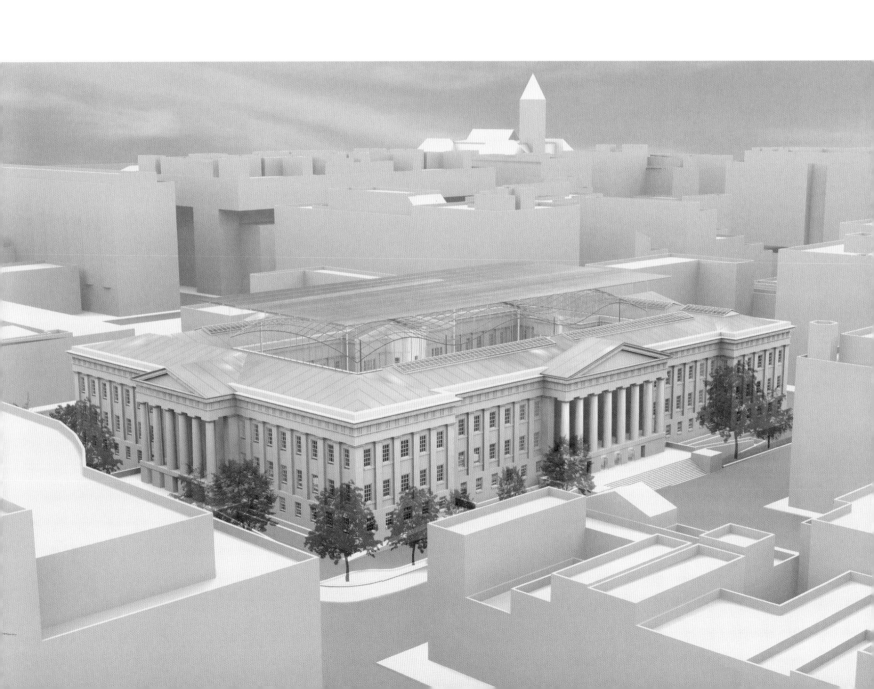

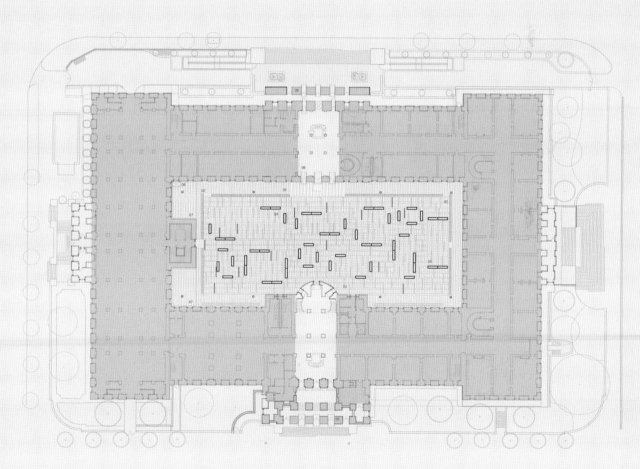

Plan

0   100 feet

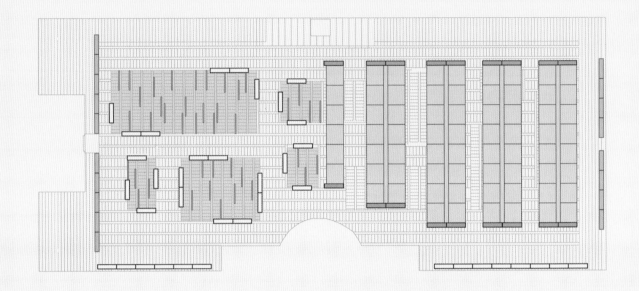

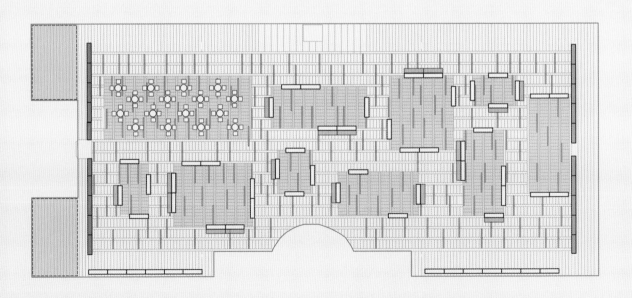

Program Diagrams

0   50 feet

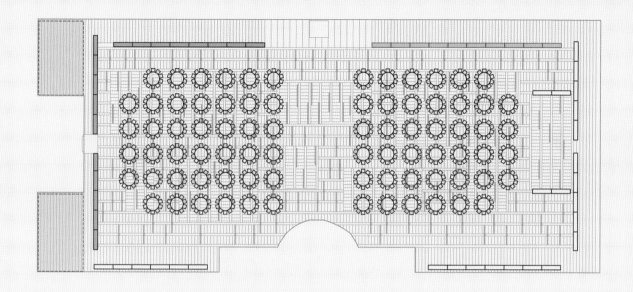

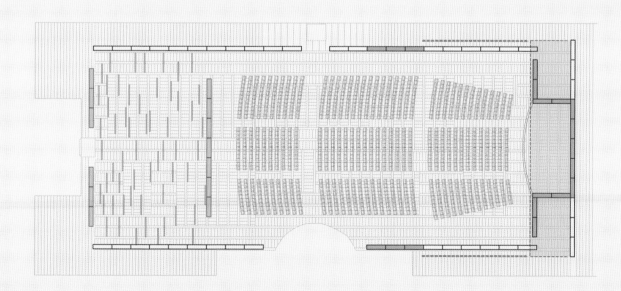

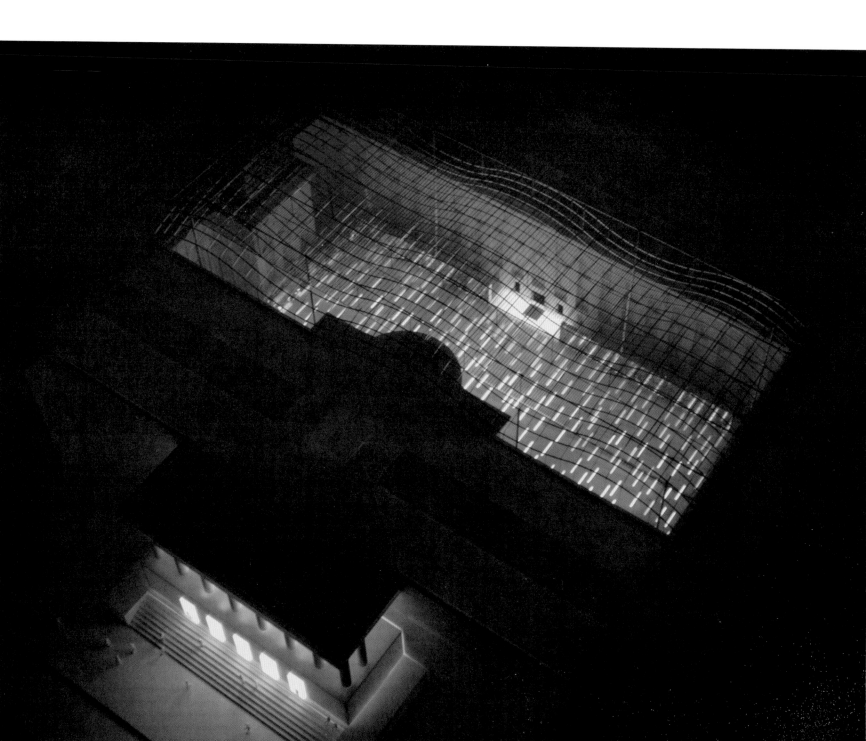

Poe Park Visitor Center, Bronx, New York, 2008. The Poe Park
Visitor Center, designed for the New York City Department of Parks
and Recreation on the Grand Concourse in the Bronx, is a community
educational facility. The 2,700-square-foot building houses exhibition and
assembly space, an information desk, learning areas, and support spaces for Poe
Park. The northern end of the structure features a large window that frames a view
of Poe Cottage, Edgar Allan Poe's last residence.

The center orients visitors within Poe Park, directing them northward toward the
historic cottage or southward to an eighty-year-old bandstand that anchors the opposite end of
the park. The building is composed of two separate volumes that slip between each other to express

the state of flux characteristic of many of Poe's stories. The two parts represent not only the opposing orientations on the site but what poet and scholar Daniel Hoffman considers the dual aspects of Poe's work: the "grotesque," or stories of horror that arise from ordinary circumstances, and the "arabesque," or stories of imagination in dreamlike circumstances.

The main entrance leads into a dramatically elongated interior space, evoking a sensation of mystery and suspense. The striking roof profile, a form suspended between ascent and descent, suggests Poe's most famous poem, "The Raven." The building is clad in dark gray slate shingles, which recall an element of the uncanny. This hard material, usually used for roofs, is layered to create, when viewed from afar, a featherlike texture. Perimeter lights in the eave both uplift the roof and cast a shadow—a blur between abstract and figural—on the paving below. The design turns apparent conflict into coexistence.

Site Plan

0   60 feet

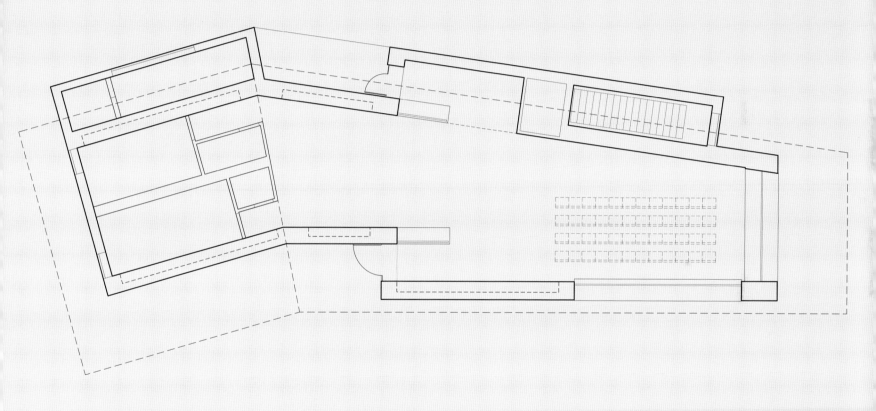

Plan

0   15 feet

Materials are codes that relate architectural design to the general understanding of civilization. They are an effective language that refines conceptual, theoretical, and technical specificity. Textures, colors, human memories associated with certain substances, surprising uses of materials: all amplify the effect, tone, and atmosphere of a project. Many of our commissions offer platforms for experiments in material uses and fabrication processes. These projects, in essence essays in spatial exploration, involve new materials and also new applications of traditional materials.

Our investigations are in the territory of materials and fabrication rather than the area of a formal, abstract manipulation of surfaces. We study how things are made or built, how new spatial formations and strategies can be realized. What is particularly fascinating is the directness of the human response provoked by the environment, a visceral reaction even in sophisticated and understated circumstances. This emotive impact can be orchestrated to generate atmospheric resonance, ultimately the most powerful engagement between architecture and humanity.

MATERIAL

House on the Gulf of Mexico II, Casey Key, Florida, 2002. The site for this compound of main house, guest house, and pool house sits between Little Sarasota Bay to the east and the Gulf of Mexico to the west. The landscape is composed in several distinct zones that gently transition one into the next. Like a horseshoe crab, the house is protected from the extreme climate by an exterior shell, or exoskeleton; the delicate inside is imbued with a softened tropical spectrum of light.

A sensitivity to materials was crucial in providing the atmospheric lighting, a neutral backdrop for the owners' art collection, and energy efficiency. In particular, specially coated plate-glass windows cast a cool blue spectral light to subdue the harsh Florida sun, and upper panes of translucent and patterned glass control heat gain and solar glare. A dichroic glass prism in the central atrium diffuses daylight from clerestory windows into a spectrum of colors that shifts with the viewing angle; at night, the atrium is illuminated by fiber-optic lighting. The glass floor of the atrium transmits natural light from the skylight to the ground-level entry along the main stair. The concrete-block structure provides a thermal mass that absorbs heat during the day and re-radiates it at night. The overhangs and windows encourage natural ventilation, further conserving energy.

An efficient long span with a limited number of pilings elevates the main house and allows an open plan for adaptability and flexibility. The generous and expansive interior of the house allows flow of movement and display of the clients' collection of modern furniture. The service infrastructure is sandwiched at the mezzanine level in the center of the house both for protection from the severe climate and for efficiency in maintenance and distribution of services.

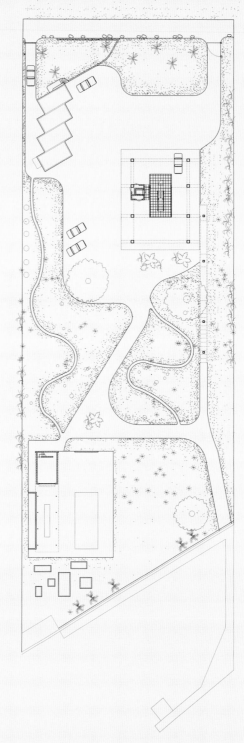

Site Plan

0   70 feet

First Level Plan

Second Level Plan

Ground Level Plan

Mezzanine Plan

0   25 feet

Kyoto Arts and Fashions, New York, New York, 1996. The store
is designed to showcase the kimono along with other traditional fabrics
and garments from Kyoto. The stepped central platform—particularly apt since
the time-honored article is always stored flat—derives its form from the proportion
of the unfolded kimono. Transactions, which always involve the act of folding, take
place at the platform, creating a central focus for the space. The lowered ceiling panel,
which conceals lighting and mechanical equipment, reflects the outline of the platform to draw
further attention to the products displayed.

        Design elements and finishes are purposefully tough and austere to contrast with
the delicacy of the wares. The perimeter walls play against the symmetry of the narrow space.
One wall is constructed of black-stained wood with sliding pegs for displaying woven cords; the
facing support is composed of etched-glass sections that conceal changing rooms. A trapeze
of stainless-steel display fixtures—used for food display in French supermarkets—exhibits obi,
the wide kimono belt, in a readily legible manner that is respectful of traditional methods of
display yet playful in its utilization of contemporary draping.

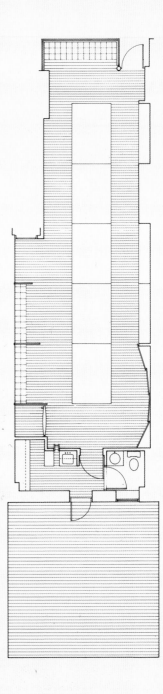

Plan

0   15 feet

"Immaterial/Ultramaterial," Harvard University Graduate School of Design, Cambridge, Massachusetts, 2001. The exhibition, sponsored by the Department of Architecture at Harvard University's Graduate School of Design, is part of the larger program "Millennium Matters." "Millennium Matters" focuses on relationships among materials, ideas, and architecture and orchestrates a dialogue among history, technology, and design.

"Immaterial/Ultramaterial" was produced by GSD faculty and students to explore what new materials mean for the future of architecture. Initial research concentrated on four themes, which became the structure for the exhibition: edge, surface, phenomena, and substance. Edge uses two historic methods of fabrication—tailoring and casting—to shape and structure thin, malleable materials such as plywood and clear rubber. Working with and against the nature of the chosen materials, these techniques extend the materials' spatial, tactile, and experiential potentials. Surface investigates the tectonic, technical, and tactile permutations of mass-engineered products, using the anonymity and blandness of common materials as positive attributes that allow transformative operations. Substance develops experiments at the level of microns, working with materials whose character is transformed by chemistry and whose surfaces are comprised of contours rather than assemblies. Phenomena addresses materials that react and respond to heat, weight, sound, moisture, light, and touch. Immaterial elements—light, sound, air, and smell— are integrated into the spatial configuration of the display area to signify boundaries and thresholds.

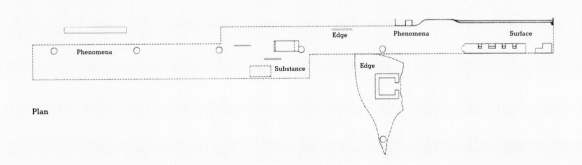

Plan

Issey Miyake Pleats Please, New York, New York, 1998. This small retail store contrasts the heavy brick facade of a nineteenth-century building in the Soho Historic District with a contemporary glass interior sleeve. By juxtaposing old opacity and new transparency, the design embraces a strategy of contrast and coexistence. The cleaned and restored facade of the 1852 industrial building retains its historic character, and a painted metal bulkhead added on the exterior responds to the recessed window facades of the neighboring structures. The new interior glass facade, a continuous surface from floor to ceiling, is recessed into the masonry walls, creating a light and ephemeral internal envelope that draws passersby from the street. A freestanding glass screen, which separates the changing rooms from the main selling floor, extends the glass enclosure around the back of the store, creating a glass box that dematerializes the restricted space.

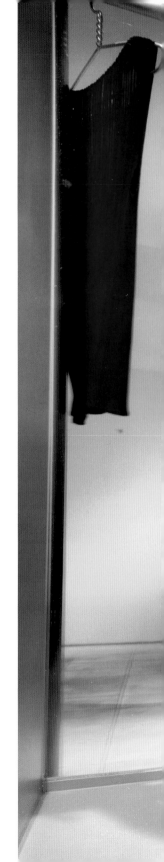

PLEATS PLEASE
ISSEY MIYAKE

Light transmitted through the glass panels is manipulated by microlouvered film applied to the interior of the glazed surfaces. The view from outside to in and vice versa transforms from obscured to transparent as consumers and window-shoppers shift position. Thus the glass acts as a medium for transforming the perception of the space rather than as a material for physical separation. The large green volume containing the cash register is constructed of a lightweight core material with aluminum cladding and is suspended from the ceiling, defying not only gravity but the small size of the shop.

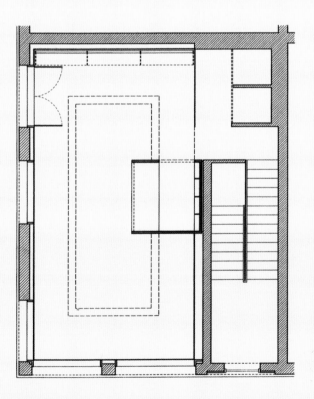

Plan

0   10 feet

Issey Miyake, New York, New York, 1996. The interior of the Issey Miyake store on Manhattan's Upper East Side—neutral yet airy and bright—allows the designer's clothes to dominate. The materials we selected are as light and thin as possible to keep their profiles delicate. Compositional elements are characterized by subtle neutral colors except for the bright yellow curtains on the fitting rooms. As an experimental alternative to the volumes of traditional cabinetwork, cabinets, shelves, changing rooms, and the parapet of the staircase leading to the stockroom below are composed of planes of Lumasite. Often used to control light in greenhouses, this thin, light-weight industrial fiberglass diffuses light with different effects when applied horizontally or vertically. Display countertops, also made of Lumasite, are supported by steel rods; these are wrapped with chromium-plated spirals to create the illusion of the play of large springs. White walls and ceiling and a light-colored stone slab floor complete the composition.

Marimekko, New York, New York, 1989. Marimekko has long been known for an affinity for natural materials. In the design for a studio and retail space, we used clear poplar wood and sisal flooring to underscore this relationship. The color scheme pairs white with shades of beige found in nature. Finishes, details, and allocation of space are simple, functional, and practical, attempting to reflect the company's products, which often express themes of nature and humanity in balanced coexistence. Gently refracted daylight bathes the space in soft northern light.

Onward Kashiyama, New York, New York, 1989. This fashion showroom for a group of young American and European designers is a venue for both clothing display and fashion shows, thus requiring a great deal of flexibility. The entrance to the showroom is a new "facade" made of highly polished plaster; reveals match the copper spacers in the Vermont green slate floor. The plaster wall exaggerates the perspective of the space, generating a sense of the monumental in an otherwise narrow room. Recessed fluorescent lighting is diffused at the ceiling, and neon lights are sharply defined along the base, increasing the monumental effect of the floating facade.

Windows on the facade vary in color, reflectivity, and qualities of light. Square windows for the offices are made of sand-blasted dichroic glass, which increases diffusion. A central rectangular window is a fish tank that is also a source for illumination. A third open window is for the receptionist. Floor spacers, window frames, door handles, and fixtures—including one unit assembled from the ready-made tubing used for plumbing pipes—are copper. All fixtures are removable and adjustable so that the showroom may be transformed into a fashion show venue.

"Structure and Surface: Contemporary Japanese Textiles," The Museum of Modern Art, New York, New York, 1999. This exhibit of contemporary Japanese textiles showcases trends in textile use by artists, designers, and manufacturers. Unobtrusive means of support highlight the delicacy of these textiles; fiber-optic lighting accentuates the characteristics of the materials, which combine ancestral techniques and advanced technology. The textiles, draped and suspended on freestanding low platforms, appear as marine creatures suspended in an aquarium. The platforms are arranged to define a nonlinear circulation sequence so that the textiles may be viewed from multiple perspectives. The textiles are ordered by their most significant characteristic: transparent, dyed, reflective, printed, sculpted, or layered. The lighting draws attention to selected surfaces, producing pensive and mysterious moods.

"Woven Inhabitation," Artists Space, New York, New York, 1999.
A temporary protective shelter, developed for an installation at the
downtown New York gallery Artists Space, incorporates weaving, a tech-
nique that is both ancient and contemporary. The portable and low-tech
shelter can be disassembled, rewoven, and reused. The materials for the project—
Polarfleece, a quick-drying, insulating fabric made from recycled plastic bottles,
and Gore-tex, a waterproof yet breathable material—are remnants donated by the
outdoor apparel company Patagonia. The characteristics of these remnants are similar
to those of materials used for the exterior walls of buildings. Retaining tactility and intimacy, two
qualities essential for everyday life, the temporary shelter prefigures the potential for wearable
technologies that create personal micro-environments and offer portable data processing with
simplified means and controls.

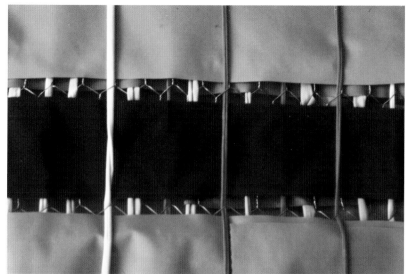

"Extreme Textiles: Designing for High Performance," Cooper-Hewitt, National Design Museum, New York, New York, 2005. Seeking to enhance understanding of a myriad of inventive industrial and technical textiles and their applications, "Extreme Textiles" brings together aeronautics, medicine, apparel, sports, agriculture, transportation, civil engineering, and other disciplines. Three-dimensional stainless-steel frames provide a flexible armature in which to view the objects. Floating in the center of the gallery space atop low white platforms, the steel frames generate a regular datum for the irregular objects, ordering the space without competing with the nineteenth-century architecture of the Cooper-Hewitt and ordering the objects without smoothing over their diverse qualities. The textiles are organized according to performance-based criteria—strong, fast, light, safe, and smart—rather than by medium or material.

EXTREME TEXTILES
DESIGNING FOR HIGH PERFORMANCE

Extreme Textiles: Designing for High Performance is made possible by Target.

⊙ TARGET

Generous support is provided by malvarm

Additional funding is provided by The Coby Foundation, Ltd., Stephen McKay, Inc., Furthermore, a program of the J. M. Kaplan Fund, Elise Jaffe + Jeffrey Brown, and Foster-Miller, Inc.

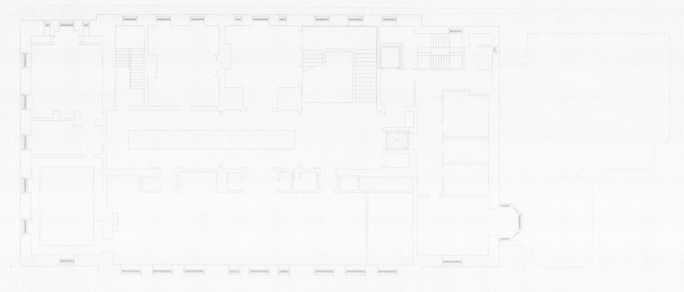

Upper Level Plan

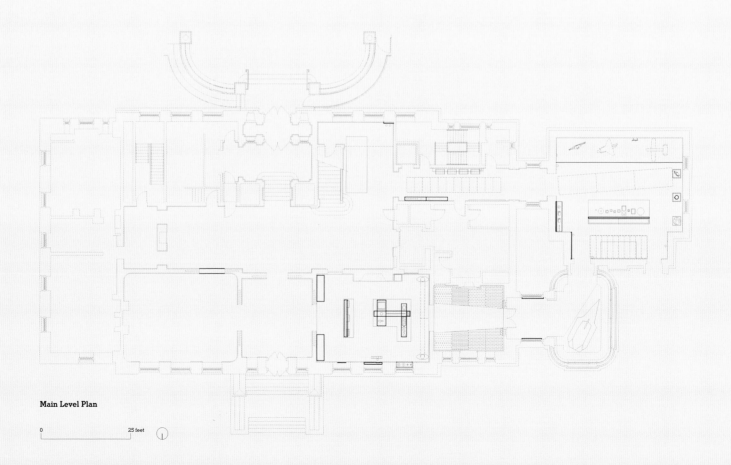

Main Level Plan

0   25 feet

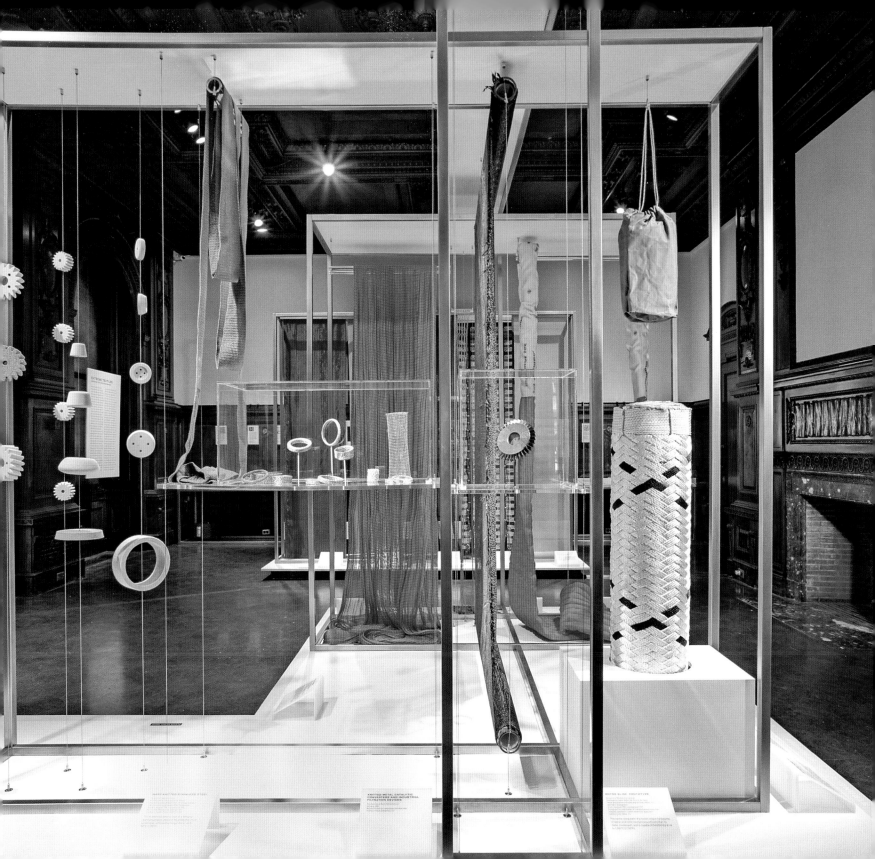

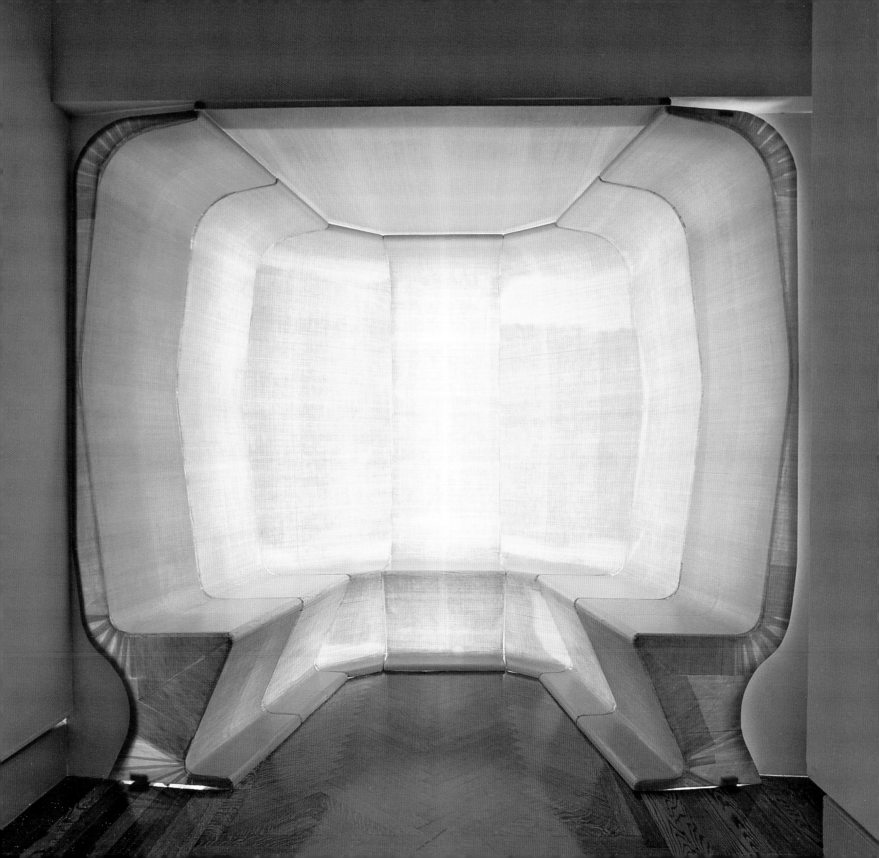

Addition to House on the Gulf of Mexico I, Casey Key, Florida, 2005.

In 1999, we designed a guest house for a Paul Rudolph residence of 1957. Three years later, we turned our attention to the original house, tucking an addition into the southeast corner of the property. The new building is attached to the older residence by a trellis; this link extends the intermediate roof plane of the primary structure and at once separates the addition from and connects it to Rudolph's design.

On the ground floor of the new construction are a kitchen and a large dining area that function as a family poolhouse. A master bedroom, bath, and open terrace are located on the second floor. Materials used in the addition are similar to those of the guest house: glass, concrete, and steel. The exterior stair, however, is fiberglass, cast in a single piece by a builder of America's Cup race boats. The ultraviolet-proof fiberglass is resistant to the severe climate of the site, light in weight, and easy to maintain. The self-supporting stair is suspended from the cantilever of the roof by a series of quarter-inch-diameter fiberglass rods.

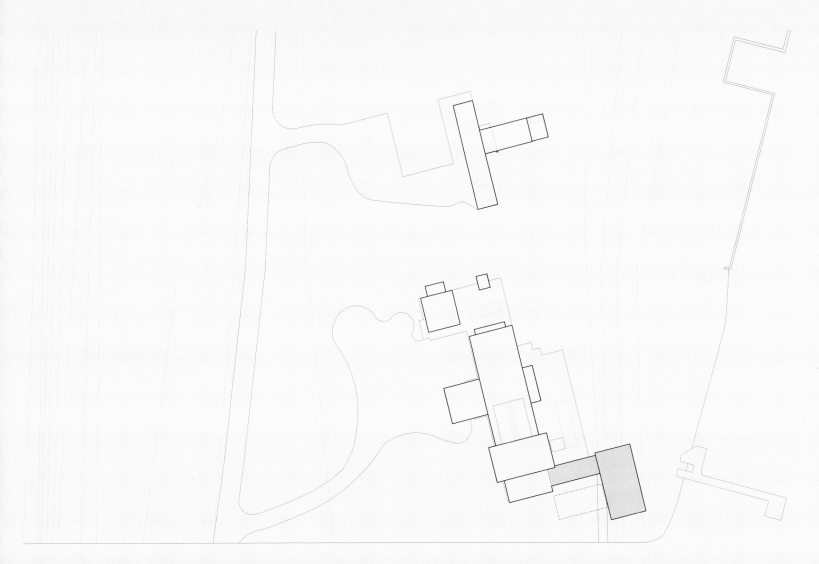

Site Plan

0   70 feet

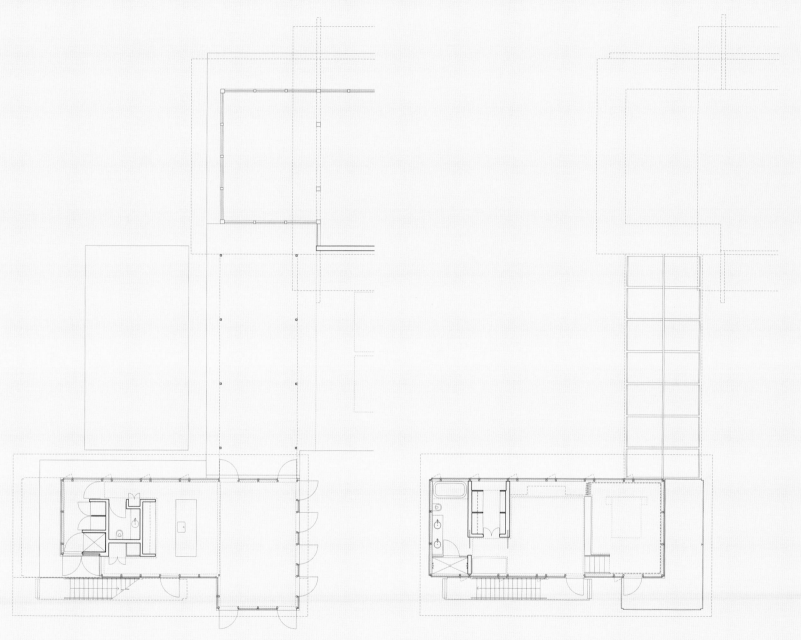

Main Level Plan

Upper Level Plan

0   15 feet

The Newspaper Café, Jindong New District Architecture Park, Jinhua City, China, 2007. The Newspaper Café is one of seventeen pavilions designed by Chinese and international architects for the Jindong New District Architecture Park. Located along the Yiwu River at the threshold between the old city of Jinhua and a new urban development proposed by Herzog and de Meuron, the Architecture Park is a public project that provides gathering spaces for the citizens of Jinhua City. The master plan was conceived by Ai Weiwei, a Beijing-based artist; his father, the well-known poet Ai Qing, was born in Jinhua.

Location Plan

0   500 meters

The building is a narrow folded plane with two facades. News is displayed on the north facade, which faces the old city, in a transparent glass-and-steel armature designed to display more than one thousand standard-size Chinese newspapers. From a distance, the newspapers, no longer individually discernible, compose an abstract texture that obscures the scale of the building. The facade facing the Architecture Park and a small museum by Ai Weiwei, which responds to the river and the new city beyond, is blank white plaster.

The design pays tribute to the Chinese custom of "wall paper": before printing was available, news was—and is, still to this day—daily displayed for public consumption, creating a natural location for gathering. The simple, folded shape of the Newspaper Café provides for a multiplicity of activities, reflecting the energy of the dramatically transforming city of Jinhua. It is a place for discourse, socializing, exchange of ideas, relaxation, and perhaps even entertainment.

Park Plan

0   300 meters

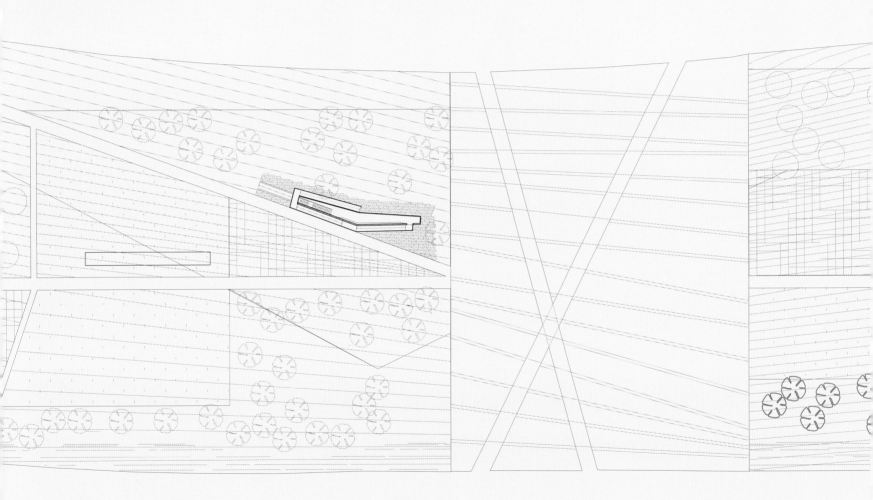

Site Plan

0   20 meters

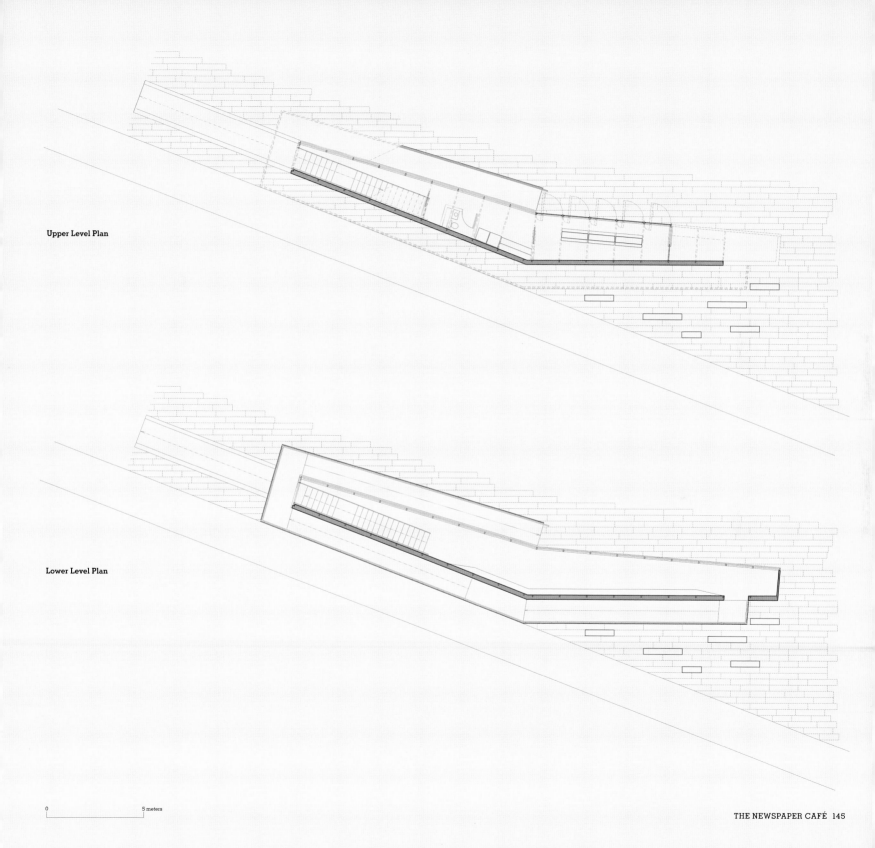

Upper Level Plan

Lower Level Plan

0   5 meters

Newspaper Module

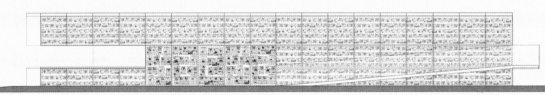

North Elevation

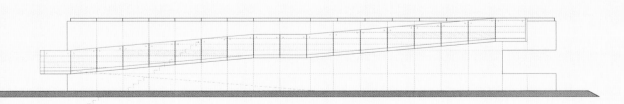

South Elevation

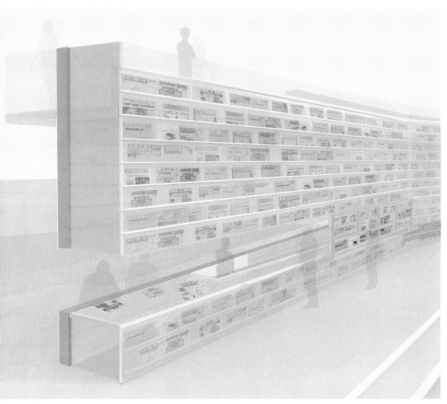

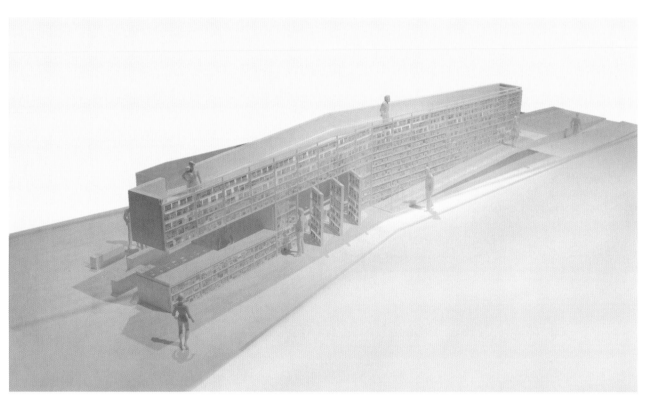

We conceive of our buildings as organisms that respond to conditions of site. Adaptation strategies occur when a conceptual scheme evolves and mutates to adjust to the specifics of geography, orientation, and climate. Some of our projects are in extreme sites with challenging climatic conditions. Hybrid elements—piloti that address flood conditions and local foliage simultaneously, glass volumes that take on both climate and historic reference—offer the opportunity to resolve such puzzles. Our hybrids endeavor to combine common-sense wisdom about siting with an innovative deployment of technology to optimize building performance. By drawing from the vocabulary of modern architecture, the projects go beyond the milieu of design language to arrive at a cultural and sustainable coexistence with nature.

SITE/
CLIMATE

Glass House Project, 1989. The Glass House started as a speculative design for a residence and media art collection in Rhode Island. A central spine/glass bridge, which bifurcates the house longitudinally into residential and art display areas, connects the house to the site. The spine is easily accessible so that the house can be transformed into a public gallery. The smaller front volume—a series of platforms and an expanded tree house in a transparent envelope—is the residence, while the opaque back volume provides a venue for projection of images of media art.

        The Glass House has become a prototype for our later work in the Northeast. To this day, the Cape Cod house, developed in the colonial era, always in harmony with its site and climate, remains the iconic house type for New England. The Glass House and its progeny provide a contemporary typology for the region. The climate of the Northeast demands a building that is solid and insulated on the north, to protect against severe winter winds and snow drifts, and transparent on the south, to promote passive solar heat gain and maximize daylighting. Clerestories provide cross-ventilation, especially during the summer months. This paradigm, expressed as staggered parallel bars, evolves according to the site and program of each house. The various iterations suggest a Case Study House program for New England.

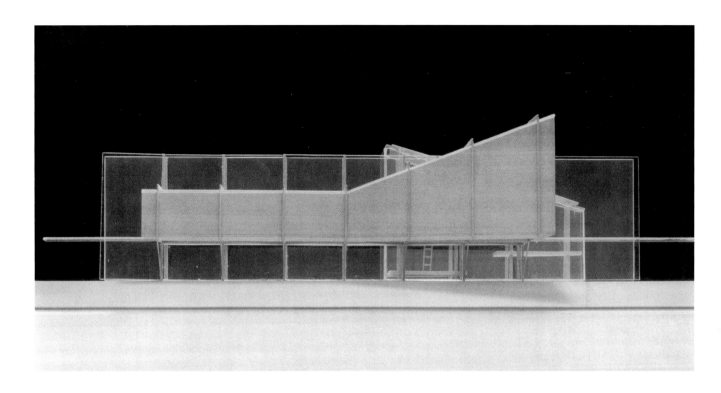

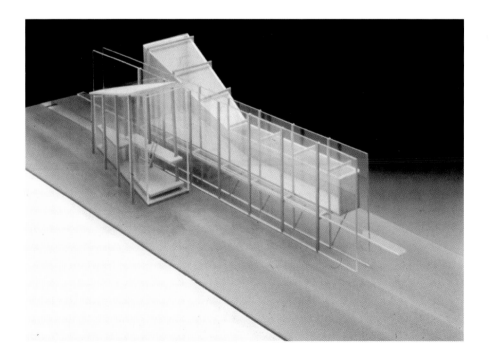

House in Maine I, Cushing, Maine, 2001. The three-bedroom house in Maine is an extension of a family compound. The client, an elderly woman, gave the original 1970s residences on the property to her children. To simplify access and upkeep, the new 1,600-square-foot house is a single story, with a ramp entrance, composed of two rectilinear volumes—one for the client's living area and the other for guests.

The orientation of the project maximizes available sunlight and views of the water. The southwest face of the residence, primarily composed of glass, welcomes the sun's natural illumination and warmth. To increase the amount of light penetrating the volume and to promote

roof drainage, the roofs are tilted toward the south and east. Although the glass facade is barely
visible from a nearby ocean inlet, the water views are expansive.

The northern side of the residence is a solid insulated white cedar wall interrupted by
slender vertical windows, which recall the rhythm of the surrounding pine and spruce grove.
The southern facade, which utilizes those same trees for shade and privacy, overlooks a spacious deck
and the protected inlet beyond. A hallway connects the volumes and straddles an existing nature
path. Clerestory windows operated by hand cranks line the hallway to promote natural ventilation.
Due to the delicacy of the coastal landscape, the house is raised to allow proper drainage of the site.

The specific program of this house may be broadened to allow the building to serve
as a residential prototype for elderly inhabitants, often living alone. It is compact, single-story,
and easy to maintain. The large expanses of glass connect daily life with views of nature, minimizing
isolation and maximizing daylighting to promote good moods and healthy living.

Site Plan

0   100 feet

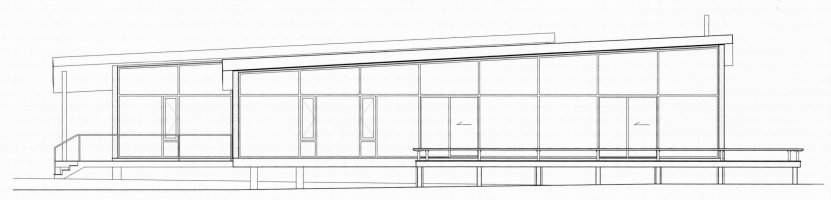

West Elevation

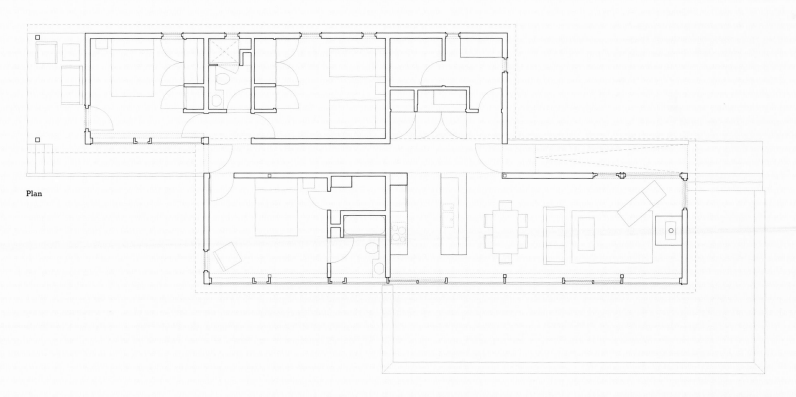

Plan

0   15 feet

House in Maine II, Penobscot Bay, Maine, 2004. This 2,500-square-foot four-bedroom family vacation house is located on a sloped open field on an island in the Penobscot Bay. The residence is situated just below the crest of a hill, and the roof slopes to follow the contours of the eighty-acre site from east to west. Along with the transparent glass facade, this composition renders the house nearly invisible from the bay below. The passive solar residence achieves views spanning almost 270 degrees; the careful siting maintains privacy, harmonizing the house with its spectacular natural setting.

       The structure consists of two rectangular volumes. A bedroom wing to the north connects to an open living wing to the south; the living wing steps down two feet to fit the sloping site. Materials and degrees of transparency also define the two spaces. The bedroom wing is clad in well-insulated white cedar with discreet vertical windows; the living wing is nearly entirely enclosed in glass, providing panoramic views of the bay. A large deck further extends the living room space.

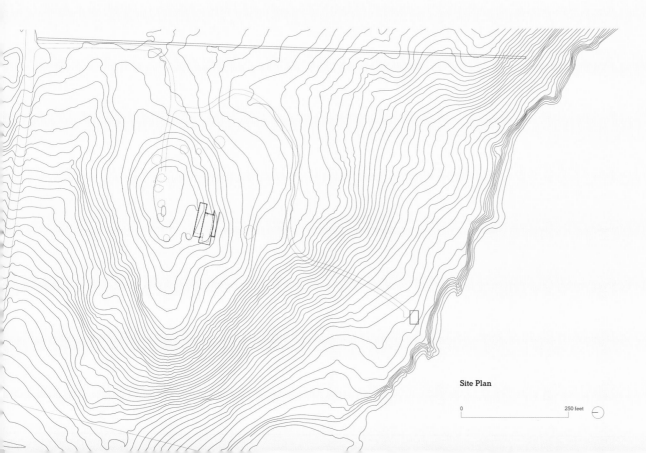

Site Plan

0   250 feet

We designed the house with attention to passive solar strategies. During the winter, daylight enters deep into the residence, promoting maximum solar gain. In the summer, heat gain is controlled by a roof overhang; harsh sunlight penetrates the house to a distance of no more than one foot. Clerestory windows at the intersection of the two roofs, windows on the north and south facades, and doors on the east-west axis facilitate constant natural ventilation in warmer months.

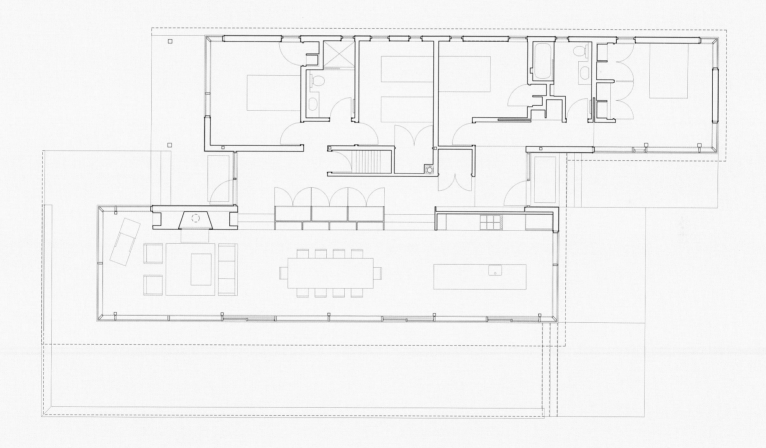

Plan

0   15 feet

House in Taghkanic, Taghkanic, New York, 2007. This house is the third in the "parallel volume" series derived from the Glass House Project prototype. The central spine of the prototype mutates into an element that adapts to the extreme site on a remote cliff with spectacular views of the Hudson Valley. The 3,800-square-foot family vacation residence, built between a pair of large boulder outcroppings, is composed of two rectangular volumes. These are connected by a central circulation path: entry, interior passages, stair, and exterior bridge link the high points of the surrounding landscape to each other and to the house. Grouping indoor and outdoor circulation along a single spine emphasizes the engagement of the residence with the unique characteristics of the site and blurs the separation of indoor and outdoor space.

The two-story east volume, containing the more private bedroom spaces, is embedded in the rock and nestled against an edge of exposed cliff face. The west volume, which holds the double-height living and dining spaces, is elevated on piers so that the terrain remains undisturbed. Glass windows along the western facade allow wide views of the surrounding landscape. An exterior deck running the full length of the western volume is cantilevered over the edge of the cliff, looking past the tops of the trees in the foreground to the distant view of the Hudson Valley.

Site Plan

0   60 feet

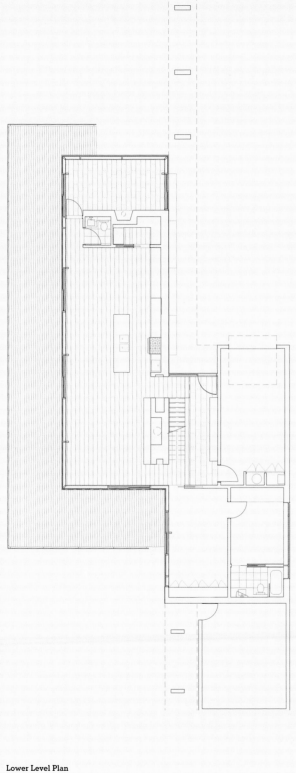

Lower Level Plan

0 — 15 feet

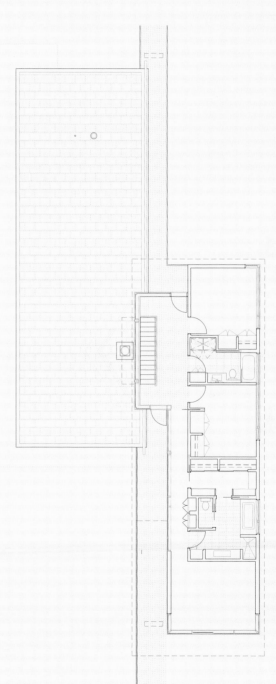

Upper Level Plan

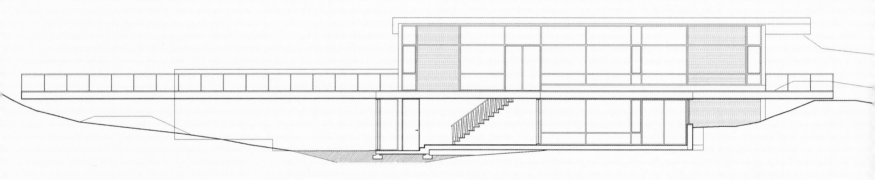

Section

0   20 feet

Salzburg Sternbrauerei Housing Competition, Salzburg, Austria, 2006. The unique cliffside site of the Salzburg Sternbrauerei Competition provides the inspiration for a design strategy of interdependence between nature and the constructed environment. The hybrid housing scheme is composed of two horizontal strata, Sky Dwelling and City Dwelling, and five distinct open spaces that connect the separate precincts of the design.

   The Sky Dwelling, hovering over the site, responds to the natural landscape; the City Dwellings, on grade, engage the urbanity of the surrounding neighborhood. The luxury units in the Sky Dwelling are suspended high in the air, close to the sheer face of the cliff, while the City Dwellings are built around courtyards, gardens, squares, and streets. Most units, narrow in depth to allow for natural ventilation and to maximize available light, have both city and cliff views. An architectural exhibition space and postgraduate study center are housed in new and historic buildings on the site.

The five types of open spaces draw from the urban structure of Salzburg, where buildings are interconnected by open spaces at various scales. Two City Dwellings frame a plaza; the western block has a semiprivate courtyard, while the east City Dwelling opens onto a private garden overlooking a forest. A promenade parallels the east-west orientation of the cliff, and a square in the eastern planning area incorporates a historic brewery.

Various sustainable strategies and materials maximize energy efficiency: innovative glass with high-performance capacity for energy and sun control in the facades of the apartments; windows fitted with internalized shading devices; a pattern of fritted glass of various densities to assure privacy and energy control. The facade treatment of the City Dwellings has a regular configuration; the pattern of the Sky Dwelling facade, discernible only from a distance, simulates the pattern of the cliff. The Sky Dwelling is supported by a diagrid structure, which combines structural truss and structural skin in a diamond-shaped matrix that minimizes material use and weight.

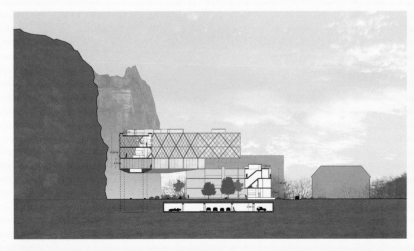 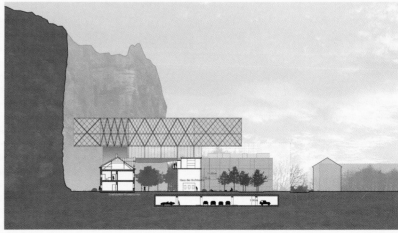

City Dwellings

City Apartment
Ground Level Corner Flip-Flop
120 square meters
2 bedrooms

City Apartment
Roof Access Corner Pivot
100 square meters
2 bedrooms

City Apartment
Terrace Access Corner T-Shape
100 square meters
2 bedrooms

City Apartment
Ground Level Flip-Flop
80 square meters
1 bedroom

City Apartment
Roof Access Flip-Flop
80 square meters
2 bedrooms

City Apartment
Roof Access Corner Flip-Flop
80 square meters
1 bedroom

City Apartment
Ground Level Corner Flip-Flop
80 square meters
1 bedroom

Sky Dwelling Luxury Units

Luxury Apartment
Roof Access
250 square meters
3 bedrooms

Luxury Apartment
Roof Access
180 square meters
3 bedrooms

Luxury Apartment
Roof Access
150 square meters
4 bedrooms

Luxury Apartment
Roof Terrace Access
120 square meters
2 bedrooms

Studio/City Dwellings

City Apartment
80 square meters
2 bedrooms

City Apartment
100 square meters
2 bedrooms

City Apartment
100 square meters
2 bedrooms

Ground Level Studio
50 square meters
1 bedroom

Student Studios

Student Studio
50 square meters
Open plan

Triplex

City Apartment
Ground Access Triplex
120 square meters
3 bedrooms

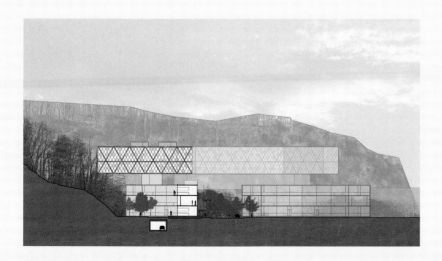

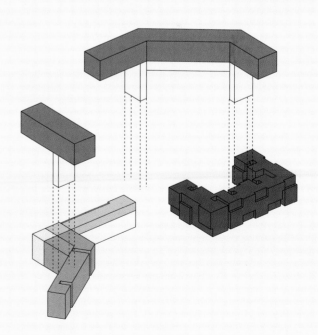

Site Plans

0 ⸺⸺⸺⸺⸺ 100 meters

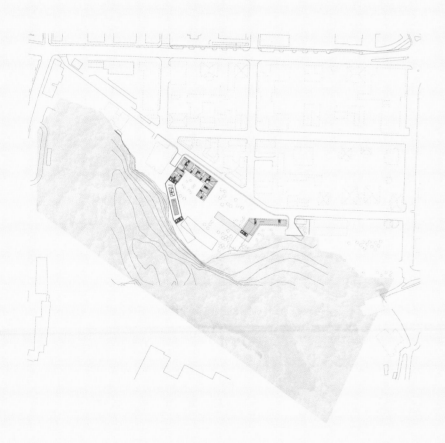

Link Hall Addition and Renovation, Syracuse, New York, 2007.
Link Hall, the home of Syracuse University's engineering school, was built
in the late 1960s next to Slocum Hall, a classical revival structure that
houses the architecture school. Our addition to Link Hall is an academic facility
shared by the university and the Syracuse Center of Excellence in Environmental
and Energy Systems. At ground level is a high-bay laboratory, a thirty-foot-high industrial space for materials testing; on the floors above are flexible student research
spaces and offices.

      Our design stands in contrast to the existing buildings in both style and substance.
Industrial in its character, structure, and material, the faceted form of the new construction distin-
guishes the program of environmental studies. The mineral-like form is a metaphoric "diamond in the
rough" that emphasizes the role of Link Hall as an emerging center of collaborative environmental
and energy research for architects and engineers.

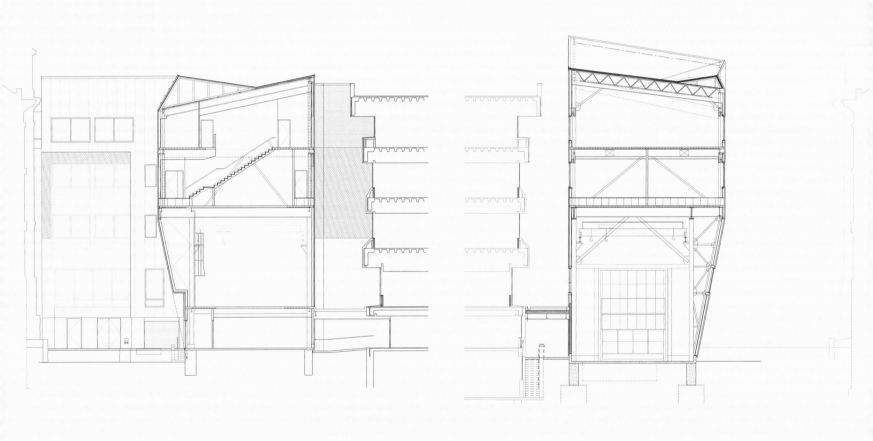

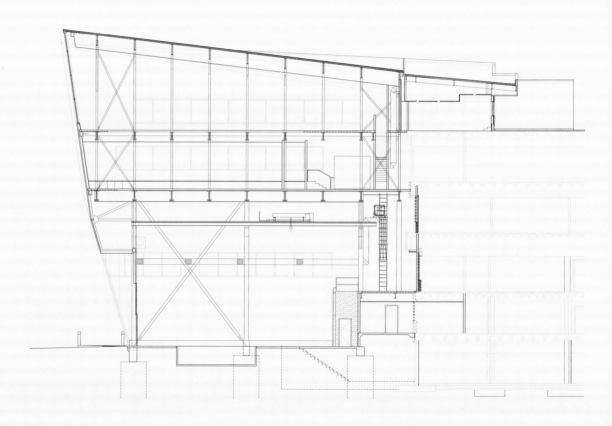

Sections

0   20 feet

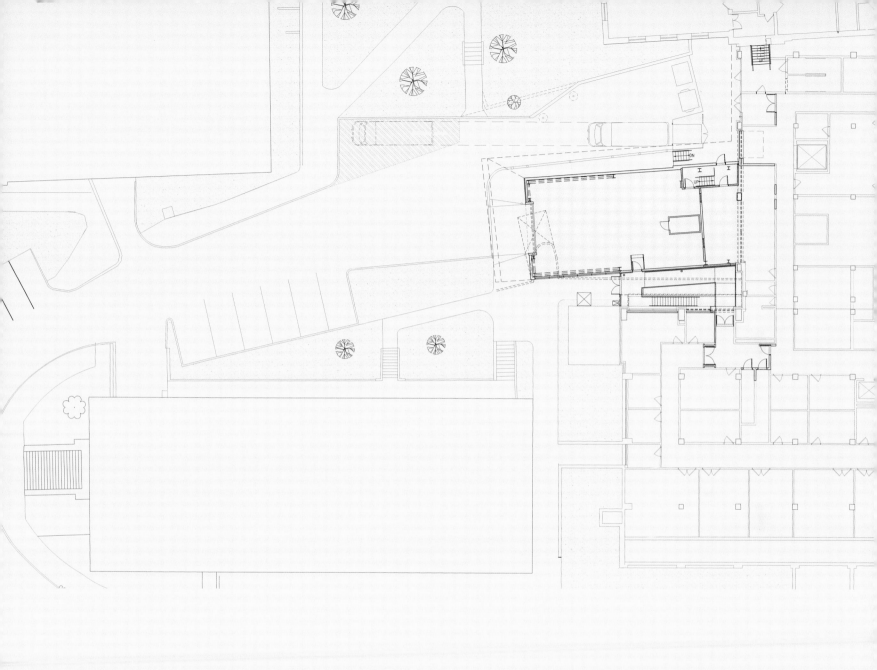

Main Level Plan with Link Hall

0   30 feet

Syracuse Center of Excellence in Environmental and Energy Systems, Syracuse, New York, 2008. This new building provides laboratory, classroom, and office space for the Syracuse Center of Excellence in Energy and Environmental Systems, a research center and a federation of more than a dozen institutes and corporations that promote energy efficiency and indoor environmental quality. Located on a neglected site in downtown Syracuse, the seven-level structure anchors the corridor connecting the city center and the campus of Syracuse University. Considered a "living lab," the facility incorporates cutting-edge technology for energy efficiency, embodying its sustainable mission

Unlike a traditional research institution, the Center of Excellence has a visible and open presence. The laboratories are organized along a circulation path that acts as gallery and public viewing space. The building's relatively narrow width takes advantage of ample daylight, natural ventilation, and panoramic views. The long facades on the north and south benefit from the movement of the sun, optimizing solar radiation in summer and winter alike. The double skin

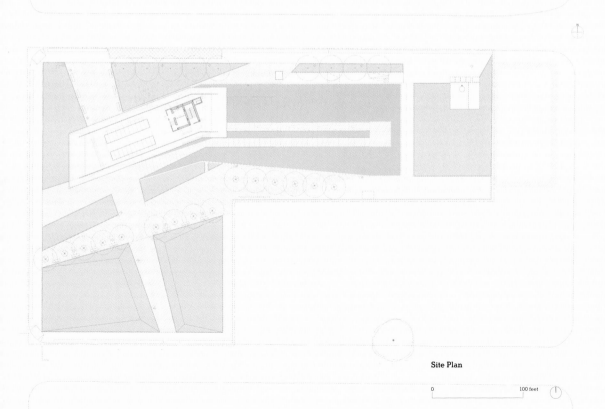

Site Plan

0   100 feet

of these facades mitigates unwanted heat gains. Overall, this energy-efficient envelope minimizes heat and cooling loads.

Sustainable design strategies include photovoltaic panels at the roof to generate electrical supply, a horizontal wind turbine, and a geothermal borefield that will provide more than half of the heating and cooling for the building. Radiant heating and cooling and displacement ventilation reduce the building's demand for mechanically driven air. Recycled and non-volatile-organic-compound-emitting materials lower embodied energy costs and foster better indoor air quality. An occupiable green roof above the laboratory at the eastern end of the building becomes a promenade to the classroom spaces while thermally insulating the area below and retaining storm water. Collected rainwater provides all of the building's non-potable water needs, with the exception of laboratory uses.

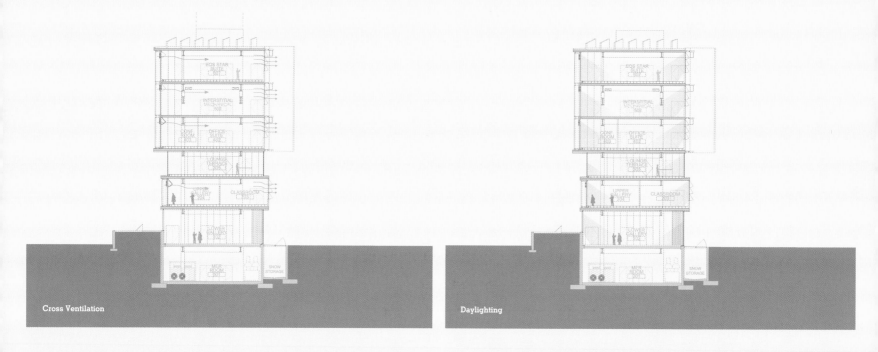

Cross Ventilation

Daylighting

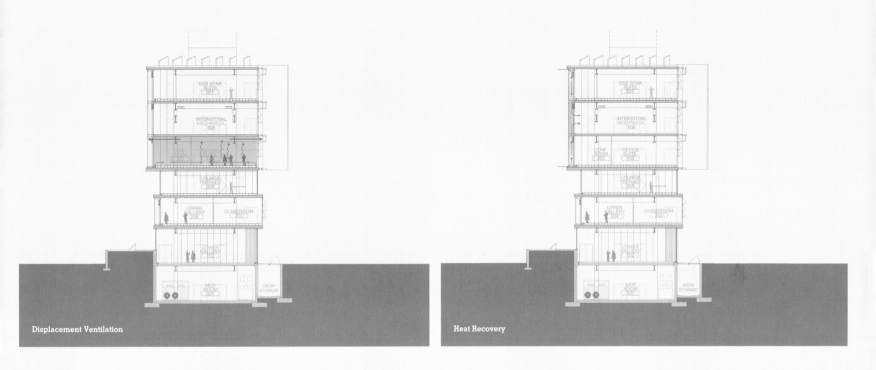

Displacement Ventilation

Heat Recovery

Radiant Ceilings

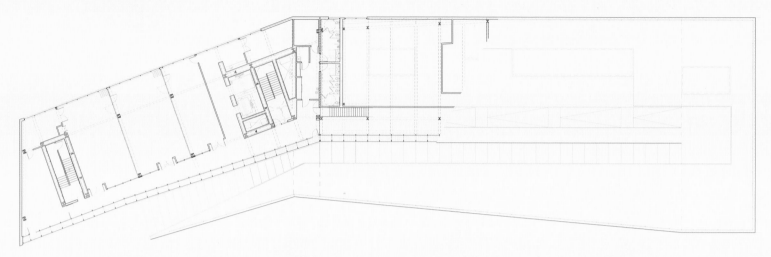

Third Level Plan

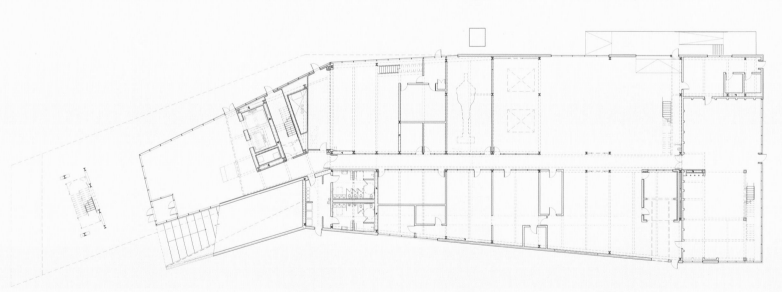

Ground Level Plan

0   50 feet

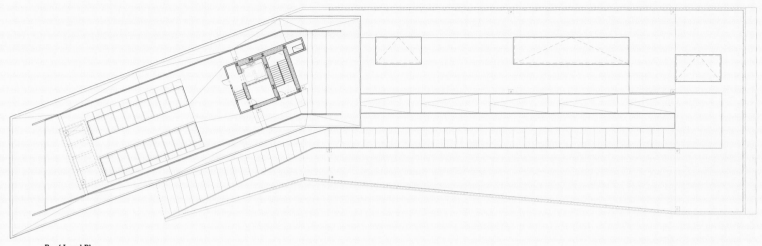

Roof Level Plan

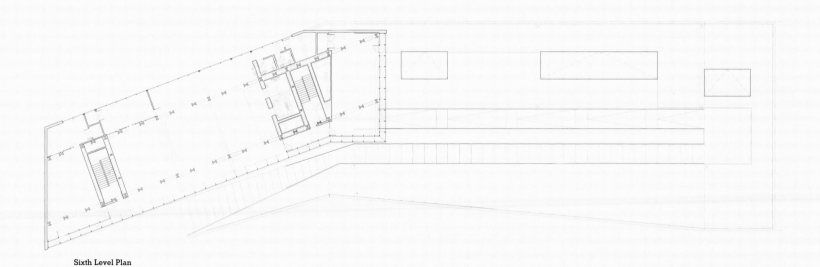

Sixth Level Plan

SYRACUSE CENTER OF EXCELLENCE IN ENVIRONMENTAL AND ENERGY SYSTEMS 199

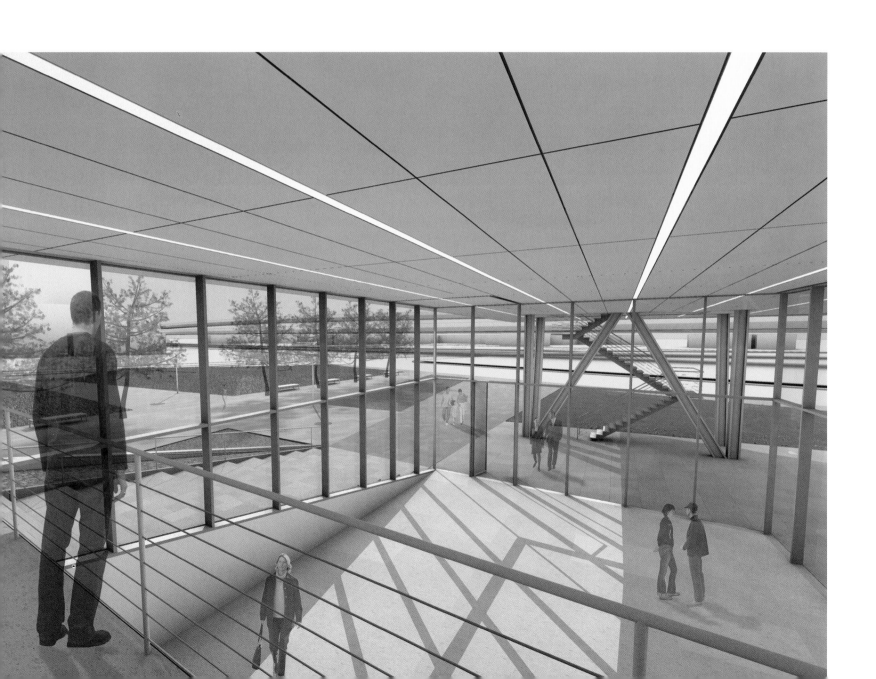

House in Garrison, Garrison, New York, 2007. The site for the
3,500-square-foot house in Garrison is located along the Hudson River.
Two main volumes—the lower and upper floors, which are aligned at right angles—
define the public and private functions of the residence. A ribbon of translucent
glass at the intersection emphasizes these distinct programs. The lower volume orients
itself westward, to nature and the river; the upper volume is directed southward, to the artifice
of New York City. The main entrance to the house leads into the lower volume beneath a large
skylight. This skylight illuminates an interior allée of ten-foot-tall tropical trees. The trees, prized
possessions of the client, underline the principle key to the design and construction of the residence: coexistence of natural and human life. Beyond the processional allée, the public volume
opens up to the river with a full wall of glazing. The upper volume, containing bedrooms and
other private functions, cantilevers dramatically to the west, beyond the public spaces below.
The master bedroom suite extends a full seventeen feet, capturing views of the Hudson River and
Bear Mountain beyond.

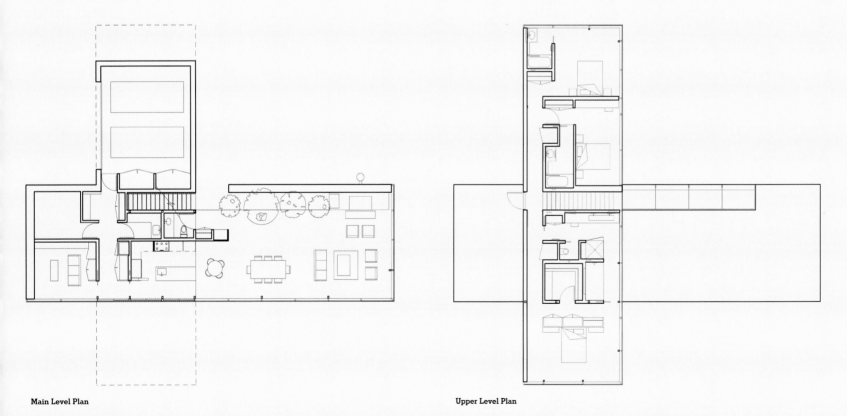

Main Level Plan

Upper Level Plan

0   20 feet

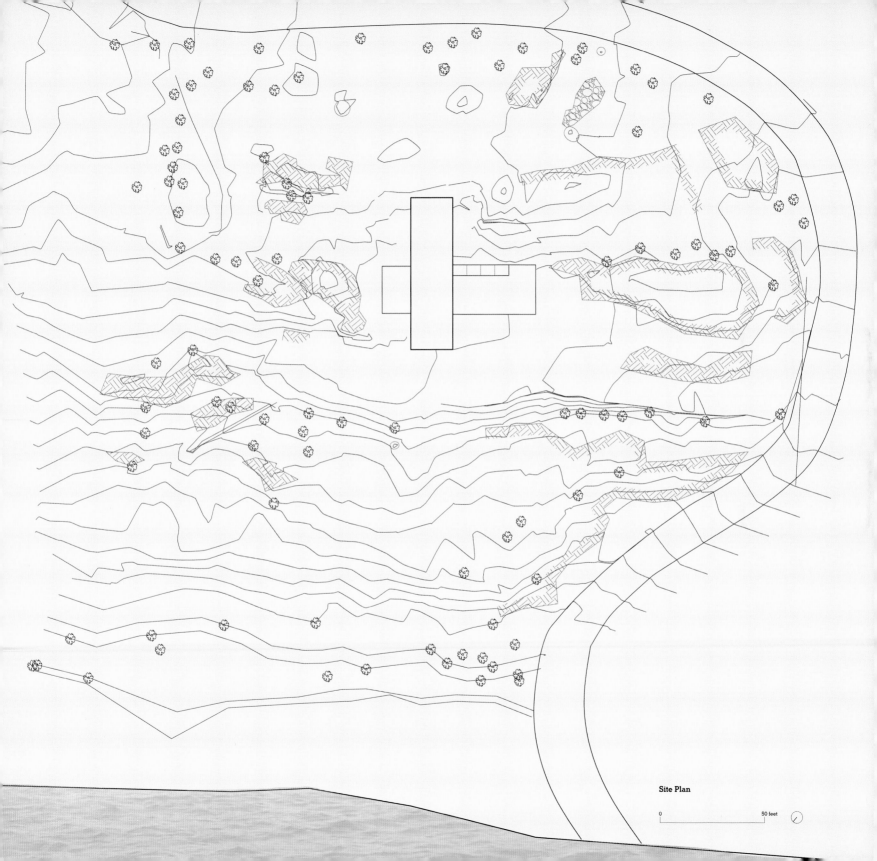

Site Plan

0   50 feet

Sustainability is the foundation not only of the design but of the construction of the house. The precise siting of the building optimizes passive solar principles, and the thermal mass of the exterior walls minimizes energy loss. A large green roof atop the lower volume provides insulation and creates landscaped views from the master bathroom. Solar panels on the roof of the upper floor make available an energy-efficient way to heat water and reduce electrical use by 60 percent. A geothermal system, which uses the earth as a heat source in winter and a heat sink in summer, eliminates the need for a boiler, thereby reducing fuel use significantly. All construction materials restrict emissions of volatile organic compounds in both fabrication and installation methods. The site landscaping utilizes a xeriscape strategy of native, low-water-use plants.

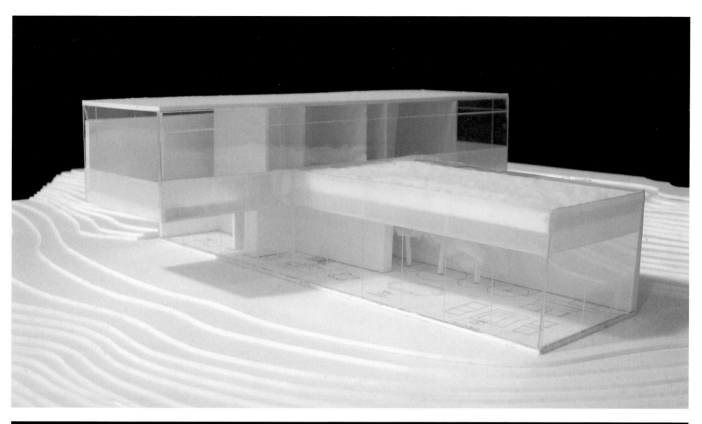

House in Chatham, Chatham, New York, 2007. Perched on a cliff in upstate New York, the house in Chatham dramatizes the relationship between building and landscape in its interplay of two volumes. The glazed western facade of the lower volume opens to stunning views that extend fifty miles to the Hudson River, while the eastern portion nestles partially below the ground plane of the dense woodland. These views of the natural landscape are in turn juxtaposed with glimpses of contemporary art throughout the house.

The open lower level consists of living, dining, kitchen, and reading spaces, which are disposed to optimize sunlight in specific rooms at particular times of day to create different moods. On the upper level, bedrooms organized around the perimeter capitalize on views and light; a private library/archive anchors the center. Discreet apertures in the upper level, reflecting the less public programs, contrast with the extensive glazing of the lower level and respond to the precise position of occupants within the house. Large overhangs on the south and west give shade, and solar panels on the roof provide domestic hot water.

The upper level is clad in recycled aluminum foam, which captures the dappled pattern of sunlight in the surrounding forest, reflecting the movement of the sun over the course of the day. With time, the aluminum will develop a patina, making visible the effects of weathering. The residential context is a novel one for the unusual and humble material, which is often used for industrial acoustic control. Transforming a matter-of-fact substance into something ethereal through detailing is a tactic that achieves perceptive effect.

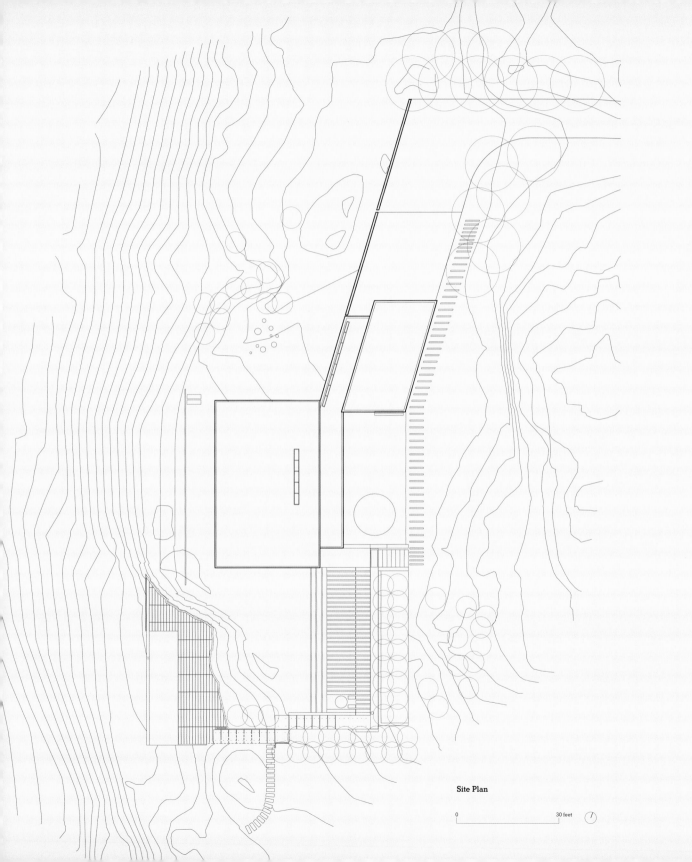

Site Plan

0   30 feet

Main Level Plan

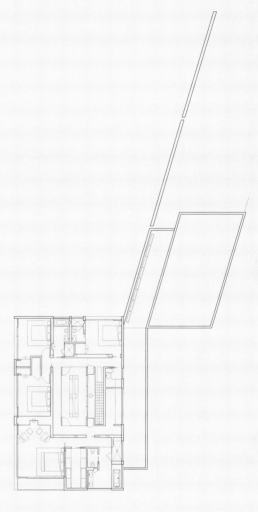

Upper Level Plan

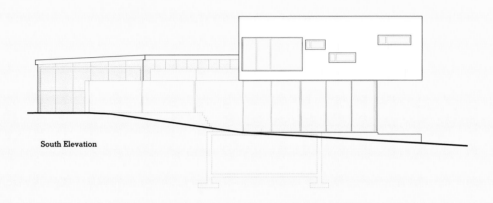

South Elevation

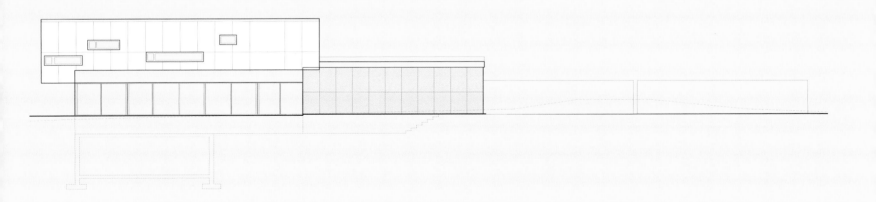

East Elevation

0   20 feet

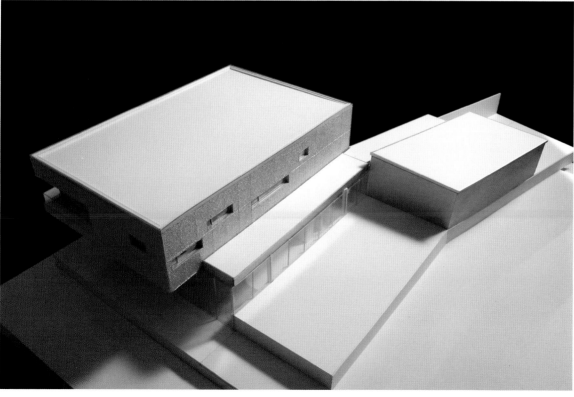

TOSHIKO MORI

Toshiko Mori FAIA, principal of the firm she established in New York in 1981, is also the Robert P. Hubbard Professor in the Practice of Architecture and the chair of the Department of Architecture at the Harvard University Graduate School of Design. Mori taught at the Cooper Union School of Architecture from 1983 until 1995. She has been a visiting faculty member at Columbia University and the Eero Saarinen Visiting Professor at Yale University, and she has lectured around the world.

The work of Toshiko Mori Architect has been published and exhibited nationally and internationally and has received numerous awards and prizes. Work by the practice was included in the exhibition "Design Life Now: National Design Triennial 2006," which was first displayed at the Cooper-Hewitt, National Design Museum and traveled to the Institute of Contemporary Art in Boston and the Contemporary Arts Museum in Houston. In 2005, Mori's work was exhibited in "Renewing Wright" at the Heinz Architectural Center of the Carnegie Museum of Art in Pittsburgh. She has edited a volume on material and fabrication research, *Immaterial/Ultramaterial*, and is currently preparing *Textile Tectonic in Architecture*.

In 2003, Mori received the inaugural John Hejduk Award from the Cooper Union. In 2005, she received the Academy Award in Architecture from the American Academy of Arts and Letters and the Medal of Honor from the New York City chapter of the American Institute of Architects. She has served on the board of trustees of the Van Alen Institute and the Storefront for Art and Architecture and has been an adviser to the New York Foundation for the Arts. She is currently an advisor to *A+U* magazine and serves on the President's Council for the Cooper Union.

Mori earned a bachelor of architecture degree from the Cooper Union and an honorary master of architecture degree from Harvard University.

TOSHIKO MORI ARCHITECT, 1981–2007

Edward Arcari
Stephen Backer
Alexandra Barker
Alyssa Sonia Boelcskevy
Bryan Boyer
Joshua Brandfonbrenner
Timothy Butler
Katherine Careddu
Jeanine Centuori
Charlene Chai
Christine Cheng
Sheila Choi
Johan Chung
Annisia Cialone
Ben Colebrook
Christina Condak
James Cornell
Wendy Cronk
Nathalie Feizer
Amy Finkel
Géza Gergö
Margaret Gilday
Charlotte Henderson
Roger Hirsch
Brece Honeycutt
Bradley Horn
Michael Innerarity
Hana Kassem
Lauren Kelly
Jolie Kerns
Michelle Kim
Avis Lai
Andrea Lamberti
Elizabeth Lee
Sonya Lee

Hui Min Liaw
Neil Logan
John May
Greg Melitonov
Chiyoko Minamizawa
Michael Morris
Misa Odanaka
Dwayne Oyler
Francine Pendleton
Cara Rachele
Pedro Reis
Aejie Rhyu
Yoshiko Sato
Tilmann Schmidt
Martha Skinner
Daniel Spiegel
Mary Springer
Jonathan Sturt
John Sullivan
Cecilia Tham
Anthon Titus
Marie Ucci
Joshua Uhl
Esmeralda Ura
Rebecca Uss
Mersiha Veledar
Noah Walker
Scott Wells
Stephanie Wong
Jenny Wu
Caroline Wyka
Richard Yancey
Amy Yang
Ritchie Yao

PROJECT CREDITS

House on the Gulf of Mexico I
Client: Betsy and Ed Cohen
Project Architect: Timothy Butler
Structural Engineer: Stirling and Wilbur Engineering Group
Landscape Architect: Quennell Rothschild and Partners
Contractor: Michael K. Walker and Associates, Inc.

**Frank Lloyd Wright's Darwin D. Martin House Complex
Visitor Center**
Client: Martin House Restoration Corporation
Project Architects: Alexandra Barker and Sonya Lee
Structural Engineer: Skidmore, Owings & Merrill
MEP Engineer: Landmark Facilities Group, Inc.
Civil Engineer: Watts Architecture and Engineering
Climate Concept: Transsolar KlimaEngineering
Facade Consultant: Front, Inc.
Landscape Architect: Quennell Rothschild and Partners
Lighting and AV Consultant: Arup Lighting
Graphic Design and Signage: 2 x 4, Inc.

House in Connecticut II
Project Architect: Jolie Kerns
Structural Engineers: Buro Happold Consulting Engineers and DiBlasi Associates
MEP Engineer: Plus Group Consulting Engineering
Civil Engineer: McCord Engineering Associates, Inc.
Landscape Architect: Quennell Rothschild and Partners
Lighting Consultant: Tillett Lighting Design, Inc.
Contractor: Prutting and Company Custom Builders

"Josef and Anni Albers: Designs for Living"
Client: Cooper-Hewitt, National Design Museum,
Smithsonian Institution, and Josef and Anni Albers Foundation
Project Architect: Jolie Kerns
Curators: Nicholas Fox Weber and Matilda McQuaid
Lighting Consultant: Anita Jorgensen Lighting Design
Exhibition Fabrication and Installation: Cooper-Hewitt,
National Design Museum, Smithsonian Institution
Exhibition Department

Josef and Anni Albers Foundation Pavilion
Client: Josef and Anni Albers Foundation
Project Architect: Jolie Kerns

Jingxiangqingke Housing Project
Client: Yongtai Real Estate Development Corporation
Project Architect: Scott Wells
Associate Architect and Master Planner: Atelier Feichang Jianzhu

Loft in New York City
Project Architects: Wendy Cronk and Sonya Lee
Structural Engineer: André Chaszar
MEP Engineer: Plus Group Consulting Engineering
Lighting and AV Consultant: Arup Lighting
Contractor: Vanguard Construction

Smithsonian Patent Office Building Courtyard Competition, *Finalist*
With: James Carpenter Design Associates, Inc.
Client: Smithsonian Institution
Project Architect: Alexandra Barker
Executive Architect: Gensler
Structural Engineer: Schlaich Bergermann und Partner
Climate Concept: Transsolar KlimaEngineering
Landscape Architect: Hargreaves Associates
Lighting Consultant: Fisher Marantz Stone

Poe Park Visitor Center
Client: City of New York Department of Parks and Recreation
Project Architects: Alexandra Barker and Michelle Kim
Structural Engineer: Buro Happold Consulting Engineers
MEP Engineer: Plus Group Consulting Engineering
Civil Engineer: Leonard J. Strandberg and Associates
Landscape Architect: Quennell Rothschild and Partners

House on the Gulf of Mexico II
Client: Renée and Mike Silverstein
Project Architect: Pedro Reis
Structural Engineer: Stirling and Wilbur Engineering Group
Landscape Architect: Quennell Rothschild and Partners
Lighting Consultant: Tanteri and Associates
Contractor: Michael K. Walker and Associates, Inc.

Kyoto Arts and Fashions
Client: Kyoto Marubeni USA, Inc.
Project Architect: Edward Arcari
MEP Engineer: Thomas Polise Consulting Engineer
Graphic Design: Ann Harakawa, Hideshi Harakawa
Contractor: K. N. Young Constructs, Inc.

"Immaterial/Ultramaterial"
Client: Harvard Graduate School of Design, Office of Exhibitions and Publications
Exhibition Coordinator: Dan Borelli
Exhibition Design and Installation: Toshiko Mori, Nader Tehrani, Marco Steinberg,
and Ron Witte with the students of the GSD
Curator: Toshiko Mori
Lighting Design: Shozo Toyohisa
Sound Installation: Harvard University Music Department

Issey Miyake Pleats Please
Client: Issey Miyake USA Corporation
Project Architect: Sheila Choi
Design Concept: Gwenael Nicolas, Curiosity, Inc.
Structural Engineer: Luke Li Calzi Consulting Engineers
MEP Engineer: Lilker Associates Consulting Engineers
Lighting Consultant: Tanteri and Associates
Contractor: Triplett Construction Company, Inc.

Issey Miyake
Client: Issey Miyake USA Corporation
Project Architect: Joshua Brandfonbrenner
Structural Engineer: Friedman and Oppenheimer
MEP Engineer: Lilker Associates Consulting Engineers
Lighting Consultant: Tanteri and Associates
Fixture Fabrication: Mison Concepts, Inc.
Contractor: Nycon, Inc.

Marimekko
Client: Marimekko, Inc.
Project Architect: Toshiko Mori
MEP Engineer: Thomas Polise Consulting Engineer
Fixture Fabrication: Mison Concepts, Inc.
Contractor: Wonder Works Construction Corporation

Onward Kashiyama
Client: Onward Kashiyama Company
Project Architect: Toshiko Mori
MEP Engineer: Thomas Polise Consulting Engineer
Fixture Fabrication: Mison Concepts, Inc.
Contractor: Meader Associates

"Structure and Surface: Contemporary Japanese Textiles"
Client: Museum of Modern Art
Project Architect: Sheila Choi
Curators: Matilda McQuaid and Cara McCarty
Lighting Consultant: Shozo Toyohisa
Exhibition Fabrication and Installation: Museum of Modern Art
Exhibition Design and Production Department

"Woven Inhabitation"
Client: Artists Space
Project Architect: Toshiko Mori
Curator: Claudia Gould

"Extreme Textiles: Designing for High Performance"
Client: Cooper-Hewitt, National Design Museum,
Smithsonian Institution
Project Architect: Sonya Lee
Curator: Matilda McQuaid
Lighting Consultant: Mary Ann Hoag
Exhibition Fabrication and Installation: Cooper-Hewitt,
National Design Museum, Smithsonian Institution
Exhibition Department

Addition to House on the Gulf of Mexico I
Client: Betsy and Ed Cohen
Project Architect: Dwayne Oyler
Structural Engineer: Stirling and Wilbur Engineering Group
Landscape Architect: Quennell Rothschild and Partners
Contractor: Michael K. Walker and Associates, Inc.

The Newspaper Café
Client: Jindong New District Architecture Park, Jinhua City
Project Architect: Jolie Kerns
Executive Architect: Ai Weiwei, Fake Design

Glass House Project, *Shinkenchiku/Central Glass International*
Architectural Design Competition, Honorable Mention
With: James Carpenter

House in Maine I
Client: Nancy Talbot
Project Architect: Alexandra Barker
Structural Engineer: Dewhurst Macfarlane and Partners, Inc.
Landscape Architect: Frederick Findlay
Contractor: Cold Mountain Builders, Inc.

House in Maine II
Client: Susan and Ivan Lowenthal
Project Architect: Alexandra Barker
Structural Engineer: Dewhurst Macfarlane and Partners, Inc.
Contractor: Cold Mountain Builders, Inc.

House in Taghkanic
Client: Stacey and Boaz Mourad
Project Architects: Wendy Cronk and Sonya Lee
Structural Engineer: Rodney D. Gibble Consulting Engineers
Civil Engineer: Dente Engineering
Landscape Architect: Reed Hilderbrand Associates, Inc.
Contractor: Rapp Construction Management

Salzburg Sternbrauerei Housing Competition,
Finalist, Honorable Mention Design
Client: Asset One Immobilientwicklungs AG
Project Architect: Joshua Uhl
Structural Engineer: Arup and Partners
Climate Concept: Transsolar KlimaEngineering
Landscape Architect: Agence Ter

Link Hall Addition and Renovation
Client: Syracuse University, Office of Design and Construction
Project Architect: Michelle Kim
Executive Architect: Einhorn Yaffee Prescott Architecture
and Engineering
Structural Engineer: Robert Silman Associates
MEP Engineer: Einhorn Yaffee Prescott Architecture and Engineering
Civil Engineer: Peterson Engineering
Construction Manager: J. D. Taylor Construction Corporation

Syracuse Center of Excellence in Environmental and Energy Systems
Client: Syracuse University, Office of Design and Construction
Project Architect: Joshua Uhl
Executive Architect: Ashley McGraw Architects
Structural Engineer: Arup and Partners
MEP Engineer: Arup and Partners
Civil Engineer: Stearns and Wheler
Climate Concept: Transsolar KlimaEngineering
Landscape Architect: Hargreaves Associates
Lab Planner/Programmer: Burt, Hill
Contractor: LeChase Construction Services

House in Garrison
Client: Carol Harracksingh
Project Architect: Sonya Lee
Structural Engineer: Rodney D. Gibble Consulting Engineers
MEP Engineer: Plus Group Consulting Engineering
Landscape Architect: Quennell Rothschild and Partners
Contractor: ASK Enterprise

House in Chatham
Client: Mary and Sean Kelly
Project Architect: Jolie Kerns
Structural Engineer: Crawford and Associates
MEP Engineer: Plus Group Consulting Engineering
Landscape Architect: Gregg Bleam Landscape Architect
Lighting Consultant: Tillotson Design Associates
Contractor: Quadresign

ILLUSTRATION CREDITS

Unless credited below, all illustrations have been provided by Toshiko Mori Architect.
Number refer to page numbers.

Iwan Baan: 59, 60, 61, 149, 170–71
Antoine Bootz: 154–55, 158, 159, 160, 161
Courtesy of the Buffalo and Erie County Historical Society: 26
Tei Carpenter: 164, 168
Einhorn Yaffee Prescott: 189
Matt Flynn: 39, 40–41, 42, 43
Andrew Garn: 125, 127, 128, 129, 130, 131, 132, 133
Brian E. Gulick: 162–63, 166–67, 169
Courtesy of the Marcel Breuer papers, 1920–1986, Archives of American Art,
Smithsonian Institution; photographs by Ben Schnall: 34
Courtesy of National Airviews, Inc.: 18
Peter Paige: 91, 92, 93, 110, 111, 113, 114, 115
Used with the permission of the Smithsonian Institution: 62–63, 64, 65, 66, 67, 68, 69, 70–71
Paul Warchol: 7, 16–17, 19, 21, 22, 23, 24, 25, 80–81, 84, 85, 86, 87, 88, 89, 94–95, 96, 97, 98, 99
100, 101, 103, 104, 105, 107, 108, 109, 117, 118, 119, 120, 121, 134–35, 137, 140
Greg Wilson: 2, 138, 141

ACKNOWLEDGMENTS

The opportunity to create this book has been a time of reflection. Its broad framework of analysis and assessment underscores the impact of a cumulative body of work and of continuing efforts to address questions as well as solutions.

Over the last twenty-five years, I have been lucky to be associated with so many talented young architects. Many of them now have their own practices; many have embarked on careers in teaching architecture. Our projects were, and continue to be, collaborations and cooperations between individuals.

A number of people have provided support, inspiration, and enlightenment, as well as opportunities to teach and practice. John Hejduk and Edward Larrabee Barnes have been mentors, John in teaching and Ed in practice. In addition, Rafael Moneo, Mack Scogin, and Jorge Silvetti, chairmen of the department of architecture at the Harvard Graduate School of Design, guided me as I took on that role.

I would like to thank the deans at the GSD, Peter Rowe and Alan Altshuler, for support and guidance. I would also like to extend, to the faculty and students at the GSD, my appreciation for their energetic engagement. Scott Cohen, Antoine Picon, Michael Hays, and Nader Tehrani have been indispensable colleagues whose bright minds and talents challenge and motivate me. My dear colleagues in Europe, especially Jacques Herzog and Pierre de Meuron, have offered a dialogue in practice and pedagogy that has endured more than three decades. They inspire me with the conceptual clarity and sensuousness of their work. And Rem Koolhaas provides relentless challenges by posing critiques and by reframing the discipline of architecture.

Kenneth Frampton always reminds me to focus on the fundamental values of architecture. He also encouraged me to assemble this book. I am grateful to have collaborated with four wonderful curators—Claudia Gould, Matilda McQuaid, Cara McCarty, and Nicholas Fox Weber—on various exhibitions. I would like to extend my appreciation to Elise Jaffe and Jeff Brown for their generous support of our projects.

I also recognize my "three muses": Diane Lewis, for her indomitable spirit and tough intellect; Laurence Madrelle, for her resilience, wit, and esprit; and Kristin Joyce, who provides infinite generosity, gentleness, and a positive attitude. My colleagues,

classmates, and students at the Cooper Union, my alma mater, deserve special mention here, for they uphold an exceptional standard of excellence.

Our work is a collaboration with clients, consultants, and builders. I am lucky to have had supportive, inspiring, and enthusiastic clients, in particular Issey Miyake USA Corporation, Betsy and Ed Cohen, Renée and Mike Silverstein, Susan and Ivan Lowenthal, Nancy Talbot, Mary and Sean Kelly, Jean Polsky and Chike Chukwulozie, Nancy Talbot, Susan and Bob Bishop, Albers Foundation, and the Martin House Restoration Corporation. We are fortunate to work with effective and collaborative consultants, in particular Peter Rothschild and Andrew Moore of Quennell Rothschild and Partners on many of our landscape designs. Two builders in particular, Michael Walker of Sarasota, Florida, and Jay Fischer of Belfast, Maine, blend an ethos of old-fashioned craftsmanship with contemporary techniques and methods to push the boundaries of excellence in built work.

I especially wish to thank Jolie Kerns and Cara Rachele, who organized the material contained in this volume and coordinated various aspects of the information needed to produce it in the span of a year. Their thorough and consistent enthusiasm and attention to detail helped to sustain creative energy for this project. Charlene Chai took care of the final checking and clarification. I would also like to acknowledge Andrea Monfried, our editor at The Monacelli Press, who has allowed us to give our own voice, personality, and character to this book. I am grateful to her, Gianfranco Monacelli, Elizabeth White, and Nicolas Rojas for this extraordinary opportunity. I also recognize Lorraine Wild, who developed the visual identity for this book, and her colleagues Robert Ruehlman and Victor Hu. I have admired Lorraine's work for nearly three decades, and it is a pleasure and a privilege to collaborate with her at long last.

I dedicate this book to my family, Tei and Jamie. Independent and artistic spirits, creative and adventurous souls, they share with me the understanding of a journey that requires the constant search for a horizon.